SHIPS

SAILORS AND THE SEA

Series Editor:
David Salariya was born in Dundee, Scotland, where he studied illustration and printmaking, concentrating on book design in his postgraduate year. He later completed a further postgraduate course in art education at Sussex University in England. He has illustrated a wide range of books on botanical, historical and mythical subjects. He has designed and created many new series of children's books for publishers in the United Kingdom and overseas. In 1989, he established his own publishing company, The Salariya Book Company Ltd. He lives in Brighton, England, with his wife, illustrator Shirley Willis.

Author:
Richard Humble has written over twenty-two books on the history of ships, maritime exploration, and naval history since his work was first published in 1971. Among the books he has authored for Franklin Watts are those in the series *Exploration Through the Ages* and *Fighting Ships*.

Consultant:
John Robinson began his museum career in 1970 at Liverpool Museum in England, working on their collection of ship models before moving two years later to the Museum of Transport in Glasgow, Scotland. Currently curator of the maritime collections at the Science Museum, John is also a council member of the Society for Nautical Research.

Series Editor	David Salariya
Book Editor	Vicki Power
Design Assistant	Carol Attwood
Consultant	John Robinson
Artists	Mark Bergin
	Bill Donohoe
	Nick Hewetson
	Tony Townsend
	Hans Wiborg-Jenssen
	Gerald Wood

First published in 1991
by Franklin Watts

Franklin Watts, Inc.
387 Park Avenue South
New York, NY 10016

© The Salariya Book Co Ltd MCMXCI

Typeset by Central Southern Typesetters (Hove) Ltd

Printed in Belgium

Artists

Mark Bergin, p 4–5, p 8–9, p 22–23, p 30–31, p 32–33, p 34, p 35; **Bill Donohoe,** p 6–7, p 26–27, p 42–43; **Nick Hewetson,** p 10–11, p 12–13, p 14–15, p 16–17, p 36–37; **Tony Townsend,** p 28–29; **Hans Wiborg-Jenssen,** p 38–39, p 40–41; **Gerald Wood,** p 18–19, p 20–21, p 24–25.

Library of Congress Cataloging-in-Publication Data
Humble, Richard.
 Ships/Richard Humble.
 p. cm. – (Timelines)
 Includes index.
 Summary: Takes the reader on a voyage though the history of boats, from the earliest Greek galleys to the modern ocean-going vessels of today.
 ISBN 0-531-15234-0—ISBN 0-531-11092-3 (lib. bdg.)
 1. Ships – Juvenile literature. [1. Ships.] I. Title.
 II. Series: Timelines
 VM150.H86 1991
 387.2–dc20
                                        91-6805
                                        CIP AC

TIMELINES
SHIPS

SAILORS AND THE SEA

Written by
RICHARD HUMBLE

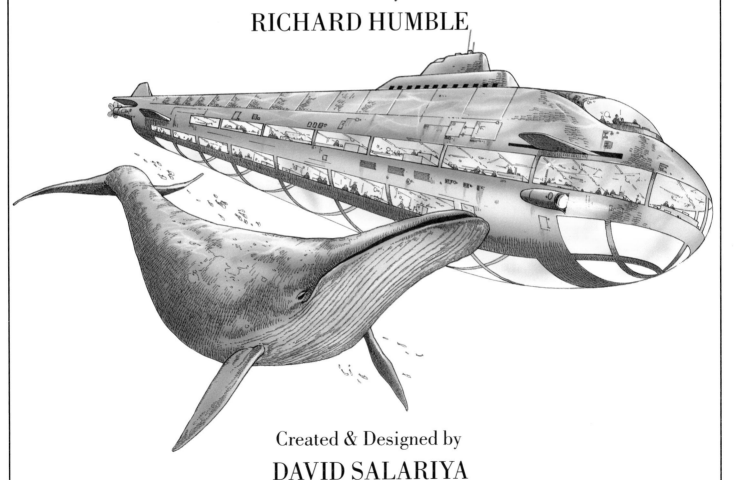

Created & Designed by
DAVID SALARIYA

FRANKLIN WATTS
New York • London • Toronto • Sydney

CONTENTS

MARK BERGIN

EARLY SHIPS

△ OVER 5,000 YEARS AGO. This is a reed boat on a seal from ancient Iraq, about 3000 B.C.

THE FIRST BOATS WERE MADE when early people discovered that bundled reeds and logs, inflated skins, and large watertight baskets would keep them afloat. Many of these primitive craft are still to be found in use today. But the first clear evidence of humans engaged in the craft of building boats and ships is found in the carvings and paintings of Egypt, from about 3400 B.C. Similar evidence shows that the Sumerians, who lived in southern Iraq, were also great early shipbuilders.

△ ◁ THE GUFA, still used on Iraq's rivers today, is a big water-proofed basket driven by paddles.
◁ SIMILAR BASKET BOATS are also used in modern Vietnam.

△ ANCIENT EGYPTIANS build a boat made up of bundled papyrus reeds. In 1970 a replica reed boat, *Ra II*, was sailed across the Atlantic from Africa by Thor Heyerdahl.

△ RAFTS OF LOGS tied side by side are among the oldest of all watercraft. This is a modern aborigine's one-person raft in Western Australia.

△ INFLATED COWHIDE floats form a raft on the Himalayan River Sutlej.

The ancient Egyptians built their first boats for sailing the River Nile. They were made of bundled papyrus reeds, very like the reed boats still used on Lake Titicaca in the South American Andes. In Egypt the only trees giving timber for boatbuilding were acacia and sycamore, from which only short timber lengths could be cut and pegged together to make the hull of a boat or ship. This kept such craft small.

△ APART FROM ASIA AND AFRICA, boats of bundled reeds were also built in South America and are still used there today — like the reed boat used by this fisherman on land-locked Lake Titicaca, high in the Andes Mountains between Bolivia and Peru.

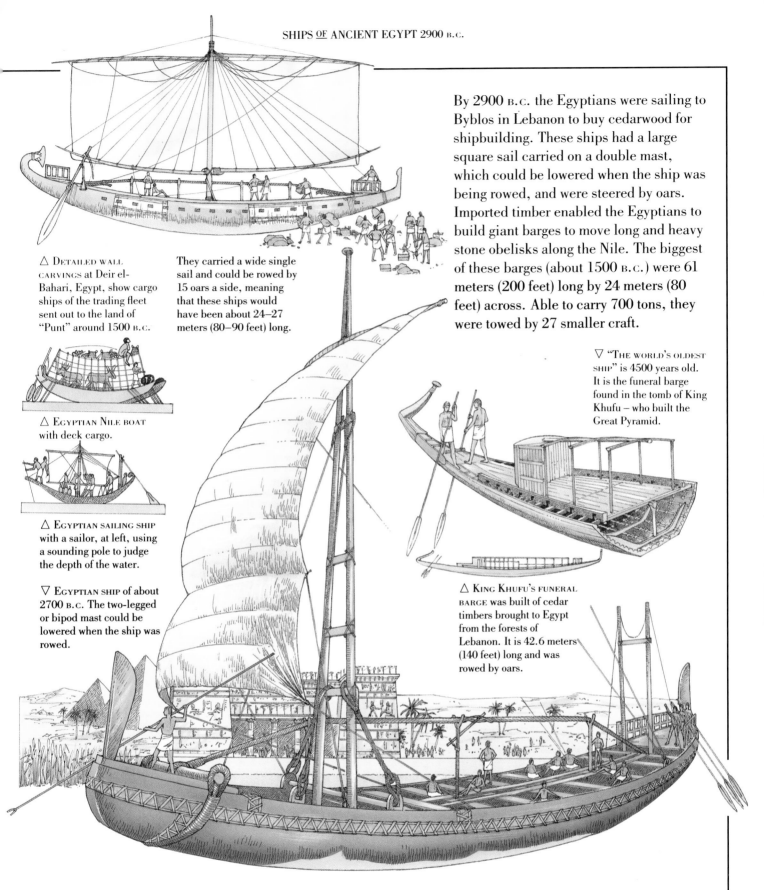

By 2900 B.C. the Egyptians were sailing to Byblos in Lebanon to buy cedarwood for shipbuilding. These ships had a large square sail carried on a double mast, which could be lowered when the ship was being rowed, and were steered by oars. Imported timber enabled the Egyptians to build giant barges to move long and heavy stone obelisks along the Nile. The biggest of these barges (about 1500 B.C.) were 61 meters (200 feet) long by 24 meters (80 feet) across. Able to carry 700 tons, they were towed by 27 smaller craft.

△ DETAILED WALL CARVINGS at Deir el-Bahari, Egypt, show cargo ships of the trading fleet sent out to the land of "Punt" around 1500 B.C.

They carried a wide single sail and could be rowed by 15 oars a side, meaning that these ships would have been about 24–27 meters (80–90 feet) long.

△ EGYPTIAN NILE BOAT with deck cargo.

△ EGYPTIAN SAILING SHIP with a sailor, at left, using a sounding pole to judge the depth of the water.

▽ EGYPTIAN SHIP of about 2700 B.C. The two-legged or bipod mast could be lowered when the ship was rowed.

▽ "THE WORLD'S OLDEST SHIP" is 4500 years old. It is the funeral barge found in the tomb of King Khufu – who built the Great Pyramid.

△ KING KHUFU'S FUNERAL BARGE was built of cedar timbers brought to Egypt from the forests of Lebanon. It is 42.6 meters (140 feet) long and was rowed by oars.

Apart from building these huge freight-carriers for use on the Nile, the Egyptians made long sea voyages for trade and conquest. The most famous of these trading voyages was sent by Queen Hatshepsut

(1504–1482 B.C.) to bring back myrrh, ivory, and ebony from the land of "Punt." This country seems to have been Somaliland, a round voyage of about 4,000 kilometers (2,500 miles).

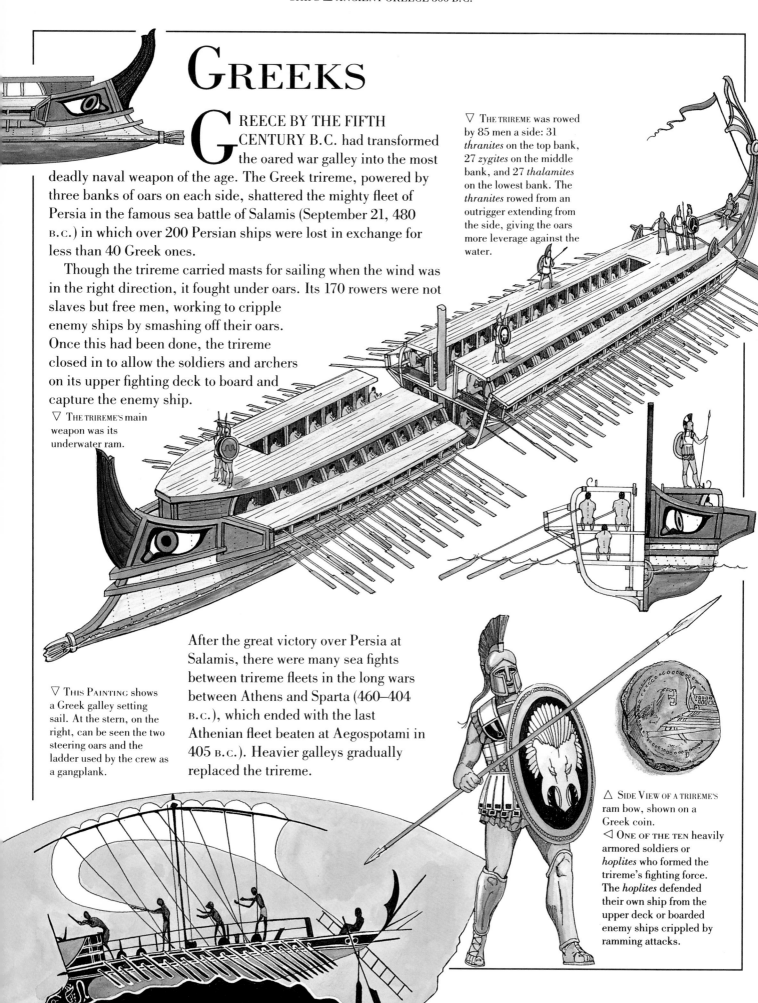

GREEKS

GREECE BY THE FIFTH CENTURY B.C. had transformed the oared war galley into the most deadly naval weapon of the age. The Greek trireme, powered by three banks of oars on each side, shattered the mighty fleet of Persia in the famous sea battle of Salamis (September 21, 480 B.C.) in which over 200 Persian ships were lost in exchange for less than 40 Greek ones.

Though the trireme carried masts for sailing when the wind was in the right direction, it fought under oars. Its 170 rowers were not slaves but free men, working to cripple enemy ships by smashing off their oars. Once this had been done, the trireme closed in to allow the soldiers and archers on its upper fighting deck to board and capture the enemy ship.

▽ THE TRIREME'S main weapon was its underwater ram.

▽ THE TRIREME was rowed by 85 men a side: 31 *thranites* on the top bank, 27 *zygites* on the middle bank, and 27 *thalamites* on the lowest bank. The *thranites* rowed from an outrigger extending from the side, giving the oars more leverage against the water.

After the great victory over Persia at Salamis, there were many sea fights between trireme fleets in the long wars between Athens and Sparta (460–404 B.C.), which ended with the last Athenian fleet beaten at Aegospotami in 405 B.C.). Heavier galleys gradually replaced the trireme.

▽ THIS PAINTING shows a Greek galley setting sail. At the stern, on the right, can be seen the two steering oars and the ladder used by the crew as a gangplank.

△ SIDE VIEW OF A TRIREME'S ram bow, shown on a Greek coin.
◁ ONE OF THE TEN heavily armored soldiers or *hoplites* who formed the trireme's fighting force. The *hoplites* defended their own ship from the upper deck or boarded enemy ships crippled by ramming attacks.

ROMANS

R OME LEARNED THE ART OF FIGHTING AT SEA from its long struggle with the fleets of Carthage (264–241 B.C.). Roman war galleys used the *corvus*, a weighted gangplank, to board enemy ships.

△ A SCENE OF ABOUT A.D. 100 at the great docks of Ostia, Rome's seaport at the mouth of the River Tiber. Here round-hulled merchant ships, with curving stern posts, unloaded cargoes from all over the Roman empire.

The long Roman civil wars of the first century B.C. ended in a great sea battle between the fleets of Octavius Caesar and Mark Antony off the Greek coast at Actium (December 2, 31 B.C.), in which the fortresslike galleys of Antony (*below*) were captured one by one. After Actium, Rome's emperors kept a navy of fast galleys to protect the sea-lanes of the Roman Empire from attacks by pirates who swarmed the islands of the Mediterranean.

△ MEMORIAL STONE to a Roman sea victory shows a warship's prow and crew.

The Roman invasion of Britain in A.D. 43 was supported by a powerful fleet of warships.

Under the Roman Empire, merchant ships brought food and goods to Rome from all over the Mediterranean, sailing from Egypt as far east as India.

▽ FAR LESS AGILE than the Greek *trireme*: a heavy Roman galley of the first century B.C.

VIKINGS

FOR OVER 250 YEARS, between about 800 and 1070, the wonderful longships of Scandinavia carried Viking warriors and traders to every country in northwest Europe, into the Mediterranean, down the great rivers of Russia to the Black Sea, and west across the Atlantic Ocean to the Faroe Islands, Iceland, Greenland, and, briefly, to the northern shore of the American continent.

Longships preserved in Viking graves have revealed what magnificent sea boats they were, with tough but flexible overlapping planking able to take the pounding of heavy seas, yet slim and shallow in draft for venturing far up creeks and rivers under oars.

The Viking ship found at Gokstad has places for 16 oars a side. As there are no benches, the men must have rowed sitting on their sea chests. The word "starboard" (from "steering board") comes from the position of the single steering oar on the right-hand stern

△ A HINGED AND DECORATED weathervane of gilded bronze for showing the wind direction.

△ VIKING BOATS HAD THE same double-ended lines and clinker build as ocean-going longships.

△ VIKING MERCHANT, with scales for weighing payments in silver and gold – often pieces of cut-up coins.

◁ SHIP OF THE GOKSTAD TYPE with mast and sail lowered. Swiveling shutters closed the oar ports when the ship was under sail.

◁ SOME OF THE RICH finds unearthed from a Viking ship burial included these items of ship's gear: buckets, pans, kitchen utensils, and a light axe.

of the ship. Like all Viking ships, the Gokstad ship was "clinker-built" of overlapping planks, 16 a side. It measures 23 meters (76.5 feet) long.

Not all Viking ships were warships. For voyages of trade and settlement the foremost ship was the broad-beamed *knorr*, designed to carry trade goods and livestock. Distant Viking colonies such as Greenland depended heavily on the regular sailing of *knorrs* from Scandinavia, bringing vital supplies in exchange for furs and walrus ivory. *Knorrs* could be docked in the harbor, or loaded and unloaded on an open beach.

△ A TRADING *KNORR*, with a cargo of trade goods and livestock.

▷ DANISH SILVER COIN shows a Viking ship with shields displayed.

◁ THE VIKINGS HAD no magnetic compass but used a sundial (reconstructed from a wooden fragment found in Greenland) for getting their bearings on long sea voyages.

◁ ▽ THE SHALLOW DRAFT of Viking ships, whether ships of war or peaceful trade, was ideal for getting close inshore on open beaches.

▽ THE LINES OF THE HULL, lowest in the midships section, made it simple to heel the ship on its side for the quick and easy landing of people and animals onto a beach.

△ THE OCEAN ROUTES sailed by Viking warriors and traders "island-hopped" west across the Atlantic, from the British Isles to the Faroes, Iceland and Greenland. From the colonies on Greenland it was a shorter voyage to North America which the Vikings called "Vinland."

MIDDLE AGES

FOR NEARLY 800 YEARS, European ships kept the clinker-built hull of overlapping planks and square sail known to the Vikings. By the thirteenth century the stern and bow had been built up into "castle" structures, and the stern-mounted rudder had replaced the steering-oar.

From trade with the Mediterranean, northern builders learned of the "carvel" structure: a skin of planks fitted edge to edge over an internal frame. They also learned how the triangular lateen sail made it easier to sail close to the wind. By about 1450 the one-masted, clinker-built European cog of the past 200 years had given place to the carvel-built, three-masted carrack.

△ WHAT BECAME KNOWN as the full "ship rig" – foremast, mainmast, and mizzenmast – had emerged by the middle of the 15th century. This is a ship-rigged carrack of about 1450.

△ 13TH CENTURY WARSHIP.

△ 13TH CENTURY "ROUND" SHIP.

△ 14TH CENTURY MERCHANT COG.

△ 13TH CENTURY WAR GALLEY.

△ 15TH CENTURY FLEMISH CARRACK.

▽ BUSY SCENE ON THE DOCKSIDE waterfront of a North European port, around the year 1350. The broad, single-masted, clinker-built cog was distinguished by its straight keel, bow, and stern posts. The cog was the most popular trading ship of the Hanseatic League, which linked major North German merchant cities.

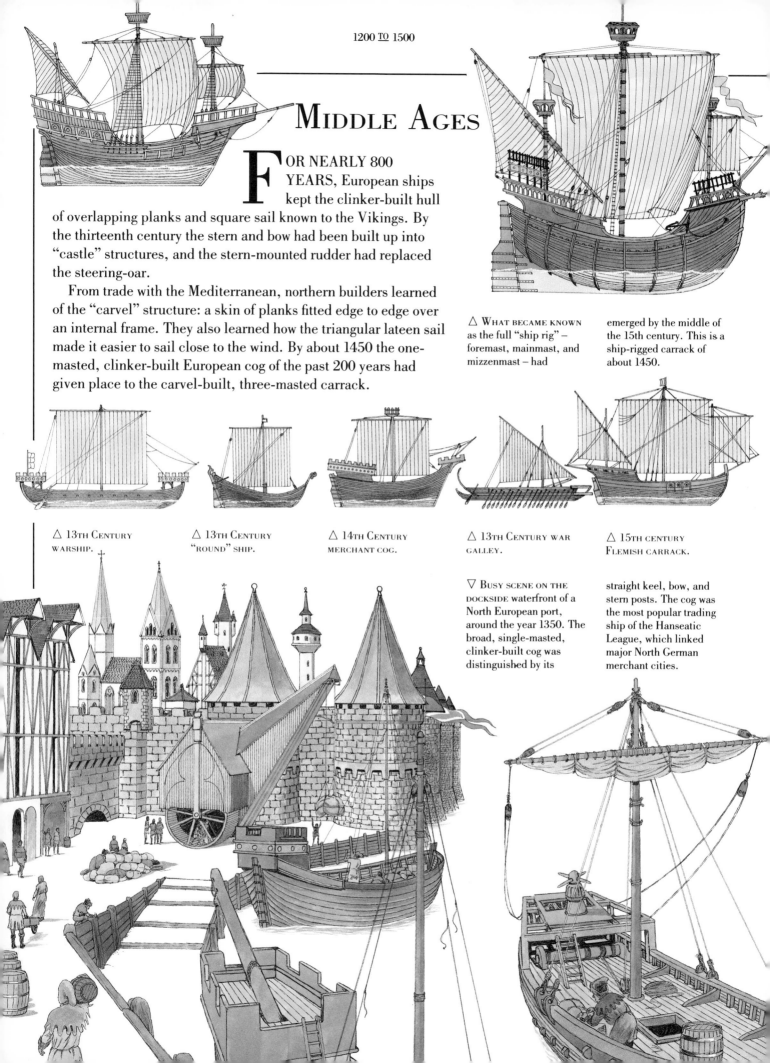

▷ ARAB NAVIGATOR using the *kamal*, a simple but efficient device for measuring the star's height above the horizon, to calculate the ship's position.

▽ ANOTHER ARAB instrument for sighting: the astrolabe.

△ DHOW TYPE FROM OMAN, Arabia – a two-masted *boum*, with a hull of stitched planks.

▷ REDUCED TO LINES AND CURVES – a medieval Arab world map, with Arabia at the center.

THE ARAB WORLD IN THE MIDDLE AGES produced some of the greatest shipbuilders and sailors of all time. Arab lateen-rigged, two-masted *dhows*, navigated by the stars, sailed as far afield as southeast Africa and China. Remarkably, Arab shipbuilding used no nails: the timbers were stitched and lashed together with coconut fiber. In 1980–81, Tim Severin built an authentic Arab *dhow* and sailed it from Muscat, Oman, to China in seven-and-a-half months.

▷ A *WA'A KAULUA*, the ocean-going double-hulled canoe. In 1976 a replica sailed the 4,830 kilometers (3,000 miles) from Hawaii to Tahiti in an amazing 35 days.

▽ THE SAMPAN IS STILL THE standard transport craft and houseboat of the Far East.

▷ TWO-MASTED CHINESE TRADING JUNK, with stern rudder, of a type which Marco Polo would have recognized more than 700 years ago.

PACIFIC ISLANDERS, in big, double-hulled canoes driven by "crab-claw" sails, also steered by the stars on voyages over 4,800 kilometers (3,000 miles), cruising the Pacific Ocean from Hawaii to New Zealand. The most advanced Asian ships in the Middle Ages were the Chinese junks recorded by Marco Polo in the thirteenth century. The biggest had five masts, 60 passenger cabins, and watertight compartments to limit the danger of flooding. The big sails were stiffened with bamboo slats.

COLUMBUS

CHRISTOPHER COLUMBUS changed the history of the world when he crossed the Atlantic Ocean in 1492 and discovered the islands of the West Indies. He was trying to find a westward maritime route to the riches of Asia. Though the best-known ship of Columbus, *Santa María*, was wrecked off Haiti, the most valuable ships in the little fleet which made the first Atlantic crossing in 1492 were *Pinta* and *Niña*, the two caravels. Both returned safety to Spain.

The caravel was a small, seaworthy type of ship which proved its worth in Portugal's voyages of exploration down the West African coast from about 1425. Normally lateen-rigged, the caravel could be converted to square rig for making long ocean runs before the wind. *Niña* was so converted by Columbus before the Atlantic crossing of 1492.

Caravels were particularly useful for venturing into shallow or dangerous waters where bigger ships could not go. Their modest size meant that on long voyages the company of a bigger ship was needed, to carry enough supplies for the crew members. *Santa María* served this purpose in 1492 until she was wrecked off the island of Hispaniola (now Haiti). A real veteran, *Niña* made at least four successful Atlantic crossings between 1492 and 1500.

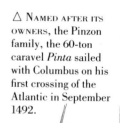

△ NAMED AFTER ITS OWNERS, the Pinzon family, the 60-ton caravel *Pinta* sailed with Columbus on his first crossing of the Atlantic in September 1492.

△ ADOPTED FROM THE ARABS, the astrolabe helped calculate the north-south latitude position.

▽ IN HIS ATTEMPTS TO SAIL direct to China across the Atlantic Ocean, Columbus believed that the earth was far smaller than its true size. The West Indies and the American continent lie just where Columbus had expected to find Japan and China.

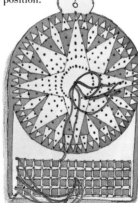

△ WITH A HOLE FOR A PEG PUT in every half hour, the traverse board recorded the ship's course during the period of a 4-hour watch.

△ A SAILOR OF COLUMBUS'S DAY. Both Spain and Portugal provided tough seamen, but Columbus had trouble finding enough volunteers for his daring ocean voyages and had to take many convicts released from Spanish prisons.

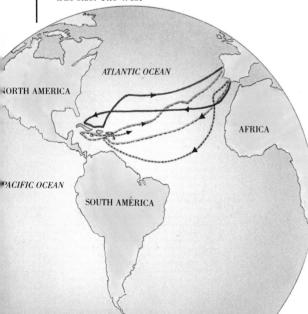

ATLANTIC OCEAN

NORTH AMERICA

AFRICA

PACIFIC OCEAN

SOUTH AMERICA

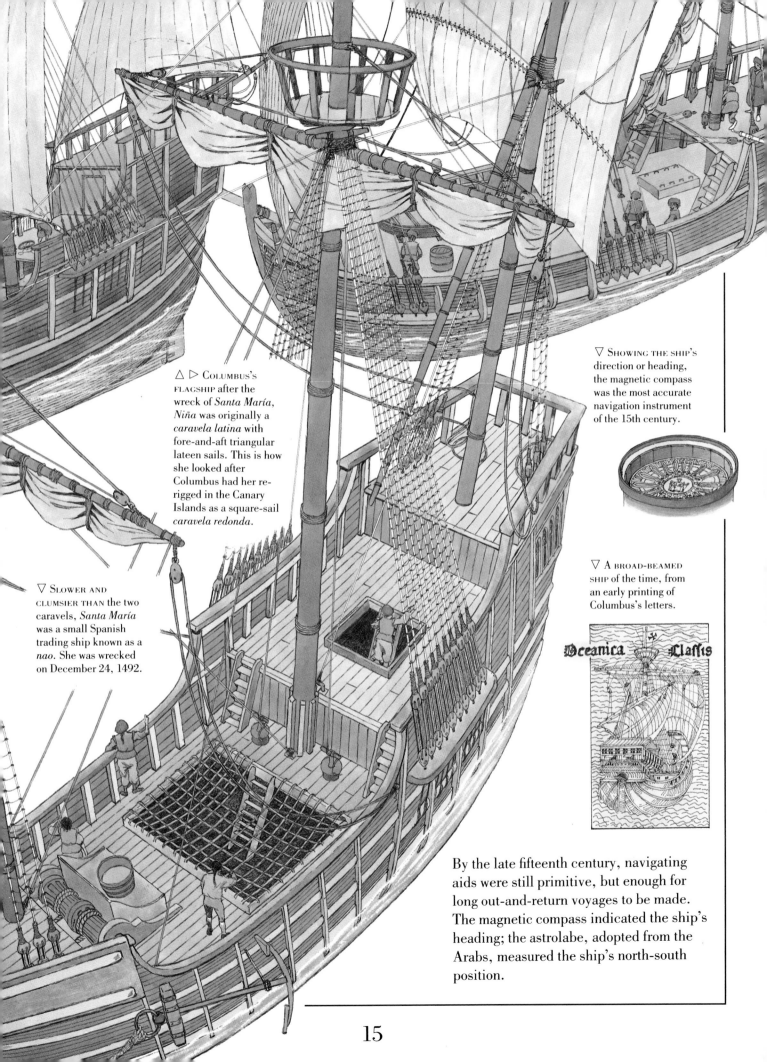

△ ▷ COLUMBUS'S
FLAGSHIP after the
wreck of *Santa María*,
Niña was originally a
caravela latina with
fore-and-aft triangular
lateen sails. This is how
she looked after
Columbus had her re-
rigged in the Canary
Islands as a square-sail
caravela redonda.

▽ SLOWER AND
CLUMSIER THAN the two
caravels, *Santa María*
was a small Spanish
trading ship known as a
nao. She was wrecked
on December 24, 1492.

▽ SHOWING THE SHIP'S
direction or heading,
the magnetic compass
was the most accurate
navigation instrument
of the 15th century.

▽ A BROAD-BEAMED
SHIP of the time, from
an early printing of
Columbus's letters.

Oceanica Classis

By the late fifteenth century, navigating
aids were still primitive, but enough for
long out-and-return voyages to be made.
The magnetic compass indicated the ship's
heading; the astrolabe, adopted from the
Arabs, measured the ship's north-south
position.

MARY ROSE

UNTIL THE REIGN OF KING HENRY VIII OF ENGLAND (1509–47), warships were mainly troop transports, which captured enemy ships by closing and boarding. But Henry VIII ordered the building of carrack-type warships armed with batteries of cannon, firing through ports cut in the ship's sides, to break the resistance of enemy ships by bombardment. His "great ships," *Great Harry* and *Mary Rose*, were the first battleships. Unfortunately, *Mary Rose*'s armaments made her top-heavy, and she sank.

▷ THE DEADWEIGHT OF HEAVY GUNS and too many soldiers in the tall "castles" made *Mary Rose* dangerously top-heavy; she rolled her lower gunports under water, flooded, and sank like a stone.

△ NEW TECHNOLOGY for a new era in war at sea: one of *Mary Rose*'s 15 heavy bronze guns, mounted on wheeled carriages. These handsome cannons were among the first of their kind cast in England.

△ GOLD "ANGEL" COIN recovered from *Mary Rose*, more than a month's pay for a seaman.

△ TUDOR TIMEPIECE: a pocket sundial.
▽ FOR NAVIGATION: dividers and protractor.

△ AN ARCHER'S decorated leather bracer, to protect the left wrist from the released bowstring.

△ HELMETED ARCHER with longbow, and a leather spacer pierced to hold 24 arrows.

The accidental sinking of *Mary Rose* on July 19, 1545 was a tragedy at the time, but a wonderful gift to history. In 1982 the buried starboard half of *Mary Rose* was raised along with thousands of weapons, tools, and pieces of equipment, giving a clear picture of what an early sixteenth century battleship was like.

Originally built in 1509–11, *Mary Rose* — and *Great Harry* — had been rebuilt in 1536–40 to carry more guns and troops. Guns were added to her towering bow and stern castles to shatter enemy attempts at boarding. Unfortunately, they also helped make the ship dangerously top-heavy. *Mary Rose* carried 91 guns in all, from small hand-held "hailshot" guns for use

against enemy boarders to heavy bronze and iron "bastards" and "culverins" mounted on wheeled carriages. Added to her normal crew of 415 were 285 soldiers, including archers skilled in the use of the English longbow. Some 139 longbows were recovered from *Mary Rose*, and 2,500 arrows. So were the instruments used by the ship's surgeon to treat the wounded.

Today preserved at Portsmouth in a special museum, with all the guns and other finds excavated from the site of her wreck, *Mary Rose* is on public display along with Nelson's famous *Victory* (*see* page 23), and the no less historic ironclad warship *Warrior* (*see* page 28).

▽ *MARY ROSE* sank as she sailed out to do battle, with her surgeon preparing to treat the wounded down below. Among the many amazing finds from the *Mary Rose*'s surgeon's chest were a bleeding bowl, flasks for holding drugs, syringes, a saw – even a wooden mallet for knocking out the patient before operating on him! The distinctive cap worn by *Mary Rose*'s surgeon – badge of the Guild of Barber-Surgeons – was found and restored.

1588—1628

△ By 1588 ENGLAND had abandoned the galleass: a sailing warship with a lower deck of oars, armed with 50 light guns.

▽ THE FLAGSHIP of the Spanish Armada, *San Martin*, was a Portuguese galleon of 48 guns.

B Y 1588, WHEN THE SPANISH ARMADA sailed against England, the latest type of warship had yet to be proved in battle. The last big sea battle, at Lepanto in the Mediterranean in 1571, had been fought between fleets of oared galleys. The new sailing galleons, designed to fight with broadsides of cannon, were still an unknown force.

Numbering 130 ships in all, the Spanish Armada included 20 of the new galleons in its fighting screen of 64 "great ships" whose task was to protect the fleet of 36 transports and 22 light scouting craft from attack by the English fleet.

The Armada was intended to fight in the old style: closing and boarding with masses of soldiers. But the English galleons fought at long range with their guns, hustling the Armada through the Channel. The Armada suffered its heaviest losses on its return to Spain, with over 25 ships wrecked and sunk off the rugged west coast of Ireland.

△ RICH YOUNG OFFICERS carried sweet-smelling pomanders to hide the many stinks of life aboard ship.

△ *ARK ROYAL*, the English flagship against the Armada.

△ GALLEASS OFFICER and overseer with whip. The need to rest and replace rowers meant that spare men had to be carried in the galleasses, all of whom needed food – a waste of space which could have gone to guns and ammunition.

△ SPANISH SOLDIERS. In some Armada ships, soldiers outnumbered sailors and gunners by over three to one. The smaller English ships were better sailed and fought.

△ WRECK of the galleass *Girona* at Dunluce, on the coast of Northern Ireland.

△ PILGRIM FAMILY. Half *Mayflower*'s passengers died during their first American winter.

M AYFLOWER, the famous Pilgrim ship of the early seventeenth century, sailed from Plymouth to New England between September 6 and November 11, 1620. A typical merchant ship of her day, *Mayflower* displaced about 180 tons, measured barely 29 meters (96.5 feet) long at the waterline, and carried 100 passengers. A replica, *Mayflower II*, repeated the famous voyage in 1957.

▷ VASA was lost in 1628 because she suffered from a serious design fault. She had been built too narrow for her length, and carrying heavy guns on the upper as well as the lower gun deck made her dangerously top-heavy. France was to prove most successful at designing stable, heavily-armed warships with the lower gun deck at a safe height above the water.

Eight years after the *Mayflower* voyage, the new Swedish warship *Vasa* capsized and sank in Stockholm harbor on her maiden voyage. Her recovery in 1961 gave the world its only complete specimen of an intact seventeenth century warship. *Vasa* carried 64 guns on two decks, and was richly decorated with painted and gilded carvings.

△ THE GORGEOUS CARVINGS encrusting *Vasa*'s stern had the Royal Arms of Sweden as their centerpiece, as she was a royal flagship.

18TH CENTURY

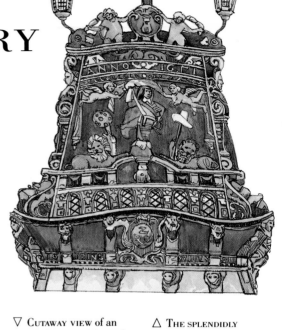

BY THE EIGHTEENTH CENTURY, the world's richest cargoes were carried by the big armed merchantmen of the Dutch, English, and French East India companies. Trading with India and the Far East, the East Indiamen carried rich cargoes of bullion on their outward voyages with which to purchase the luxury goods demanded by the markets of Europe – spices, tea, Chinese porcelain and jade, jewelry, and furniture. The cargoes carried by a single East Indiaman would have made every man in her crew rich for life, and had to be defended against pirates. East Indiamen were therefore as heavily armed as many warships, with up to 50 guns or more per ship, and indeed many did serve as warships in time of war.

▽ CUTAWAY VIEW of an East Indiaman of the 18th century, showing decks and living spaces.

△ THE SPLENDIDLY ORNAMENTED stern transom of the Dutch East Indiaman *Prins Willem*.

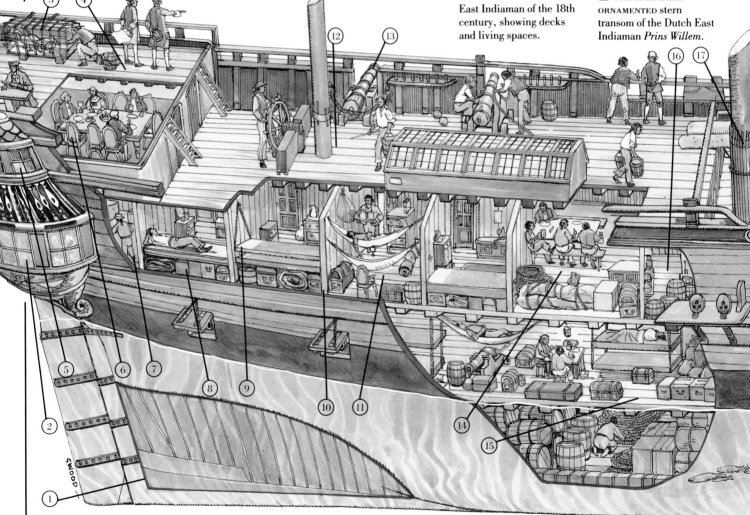

1 Junction of keel, stern post, and rudder.
2 Quarter gallery outside stern cabins and saloon.
3 Coop for live poultry.
4 Upper or poopdeck.
5 Roundhouse cabins.
6 Cuddy, or dining saloon.
7 Stern or "Great" Cabin.
8 Cabins.
9 Cabins with hanging cots.
10 Partition.
11 Cabin with slung hammocks.
12 Quarterdeck.
13 18-pounder cannon.
14 Maindeck steerage.
15 Lower Deck steerage living area.

There are plenty of detailed ship models in museums which show what East Indiamen looked like. Rather less was known about their cargoes until wrecked East Indiamen were found and excavated by divers over the past 30 years. Two such wrecks are those of the Dutch East Indiaman *Witte Leeuw* (sunk off St. Helena in 1613), and *Slot ter Hooge* (sunk off the Madeira Islands in 1724). *Witte Leeuw* was homeward bound from the East Indies with a cargo of 1,311 diamonds, spices, and Chinese porcelain. A century later, outward bound from Holland to the East Indies, *Slot ter Hooge*'s cargo consisted of three tons of silver ingots and four chests full of silver coins.

The splendid era of the stately East Indiamen was a long one. It lasted nearly

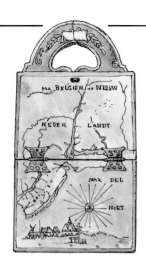

△ 17TH CENTURY MAP of the sea approaches to the Dutch American colony "New Holland" – afterwards New York.
▷ RELIC OF THE RICH China tea trade – figurine of a Chinese tea porter.

250 years until the 1840s and 1850s, when private merchant shipping fleets helped by steam power proved able to ship cargoes faster and more cheaply.

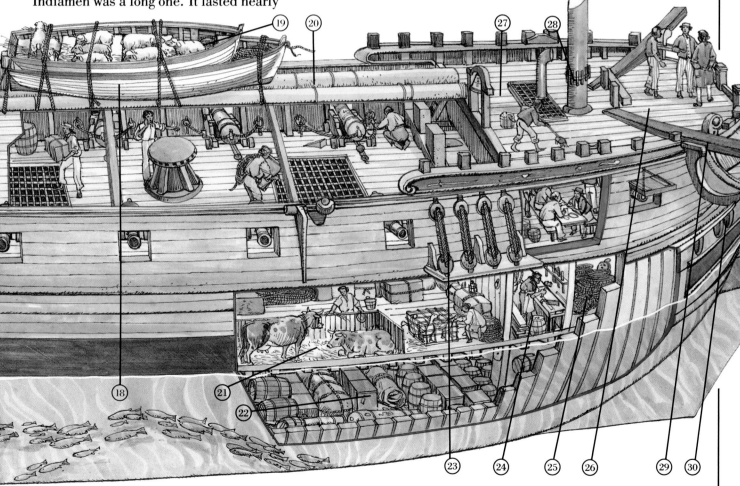

16 Food storage pantry.
17 Pikes for fighting off enemy boarders.
18 Ship's boats.
19 Boat used as sheep pen.
20 Spare spars.
21 Cattle pen.
22 Dismantled guns.
23 Chains – platform for heaving the sounding-lead in shallow water.
24 Carpenter's workshop.
25 Boatswain's stores.
26 Forecastle.
27 Forecastle deck.
28 Rack of belaying pins.
29 Cathead.
30 Anchor cable hawsehole.

1650 TO 1850

ESTABLISHED BY THE MID-SEVENTEENTH CENTURY as the most powerful type of sailing battleship, the *ship of the line* remained supreme until the coming of steam and armor plate in the late 1850s. Ships of the line were heavy warships considered, by the number of their guns, strong enough to join the line of battle: the fighting fleet formation in which the biggest number of heavy guns could be brought to bear on the ships of the enemy fleet.

By the middle eighteenth century, ships of the line were rated by their gun totals. A three-decked *First Rate* carried 100 guns or more. The biggest ever built was Spain's *Santissima Trinidad* of 136 guns, sunk after Trafalgar in 1805. Then came *Second Rates* (84–100 guns), *Third Rates* (70–84 guns) and *Fourth Rates* (50–70 guns). By the French wars of 1792–1815, the standard ship of the line was the two-decked Third Rate of 74 guns, with a crew of about 450 men.

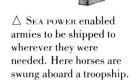

△ SEA POWER enabled armies to be shipped to wherever they were needed. Here horses are swung aboard a troopship.

▽ BREAKING THE ENEMY line broke up the enemy fleet into small units for easier destruction in battle.

△ LOADING. After the powder charge had been rammed in and held by a felt "wad," the shot followed and was also fixed with a wad before the gun was fired.

In battle, a ship of the line's rate of fire and crew's fighting spirit were always more important than ship size or number of guns. At Cape St. Vincent (February 14, 1797), Nelson's 74-gun *Captain*, though badly damaged, took both the Spanish *San Nicolas* and *San Josef* by running alongside and boarding.

◁ OFFICERS: a captain (left) and a lieutenant.
▷ A MIDSHIPMAN, with speaking trumpet and a boy "powder monkey" who supplied the guns.

◁ THE SHIP'S TOILETS, up in the bows, were kept clean by the sea.
▷ A SEAMAN'S "dinner": hard biscuit, cheese, boiled salt meat, and a ration of water.

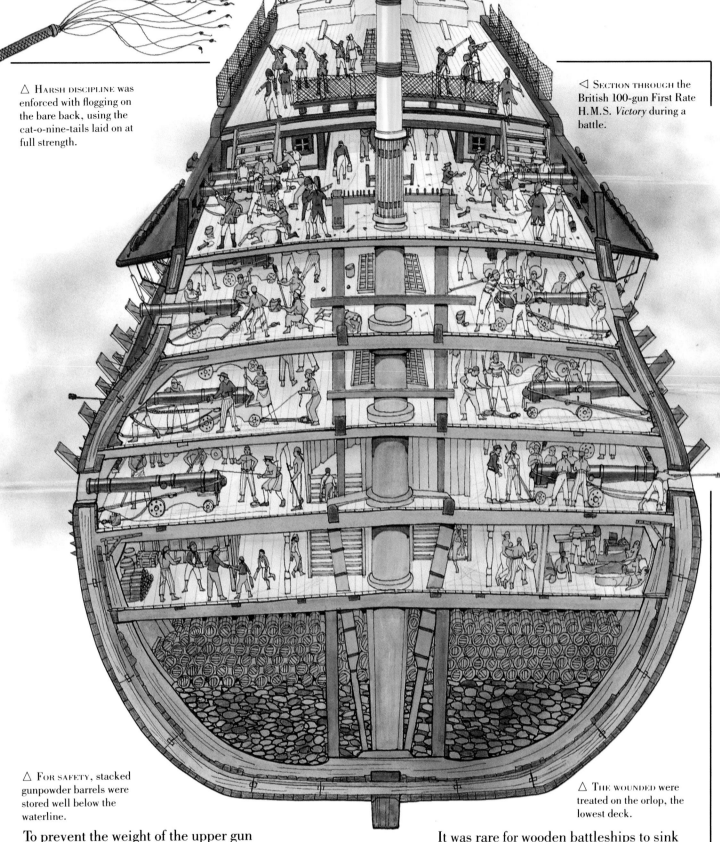

△ HARSH DISCIPLINE was enforced with flogging on the bare back, using the cat-o-nine-tails laid on at full strength.

◁ SECTION THROUGH the British 100-gun First Rate H.M.S. *Victory* during a battle.

△ FOR SAFETY, stacked gunpowder barrels were stored well below the waterline.

△ THE WOUNDED were treated on the orlop, the lowest deck.

To prevent the weight of the upper gun decks from making the ship top-heavy, the ship was built with a sharp "tumble-home," or inward sloping of the sides. In *Victory* the heaviest guns were carried on the lower gun deck (32-pounders), with 24-pounders on the middle gun deck and 12-pounders on the upper gun deck.

▽ SOLID ROUNDSHOT, types of disabling shot, and grapeshot.

It was rare for wooden battleships to sink each other in battle. They tried to batter enemy ships into wrecks for capture by boarding. Apart from solid roundshot, the guns could fire whirling "disabling shot" for slicing enemy rigging, and "grapeshot" for cutting down large numbers of men.

THE PACIFIC

THE THREE VOYAGES of Captain James Cook (1768–71, 1772–75, and 1776–79) mapped the Pacific Ocean from Cape Horn to Australia, from the Antarctic to Alaska. Helped by accurate new clockwork time-keepers to measure the ship's east-west longitude, they added more details to the map of the world than has ever been done in the space of 11 years.

Like those of the great explorers before him, Cook's voyages were not made in specially-designed vessels but in ordinary merchant ships of the time. Cook's two famous ships, the *Endeavour* of his first voyage and the *Resolution* of his second and third voyages, were sturdy colliers built for the North Sea coal trade, known as "Whitby cats."

Cook's *Endeavour* was the former collier *Earl of Pembroke*, rerigged and rebuilt with extra cabins for the officers and scientists she was to carry, and given an outer protective skin of planking to resist attack by the wood-boring worms of tropic seas. This outer skin was fastened in

△ RELIC OF A NEW AGE OF accuracy in ocean navigation, mentioned in Charles Dickens's book *Dombey and Son*, this wooden midshipman holding a sextant was a shop sign for a maker and seller of charts and instruments in London.

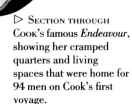

▷ POCKET GLOBE OF 1790 shows the track of *Endeavour* in 1768–1771. The inside of the carrying-case shows the stars of the Northern and Southern hemispheres.

▷ SECTION THROUGH Cook's famous *Endeavour*, showing her cramped quarters and living spaces that were home for 94 men on Cook's first voyage.

◁ APART FROM HIS DISCOVERIES, Cook proved that with proper health care and nutrition it was possible to sail around the world without a single man dying from disease aboard ship.

▷ WHEN PUBLISHED, Cook's journal became a best-seller. These pages show birds and a tattooed Maori warrior from New Zealand, discovered by Cook in October 1769.

INDIAN OCEAN

ASIA

AFRICA

NORTH AMERICA

ATLANTIC OCEAN

AUSTRALIA

PACIFIC OCEAN

SOUTH AMERICA

INDIAN OCEAN

ANTARCTICA

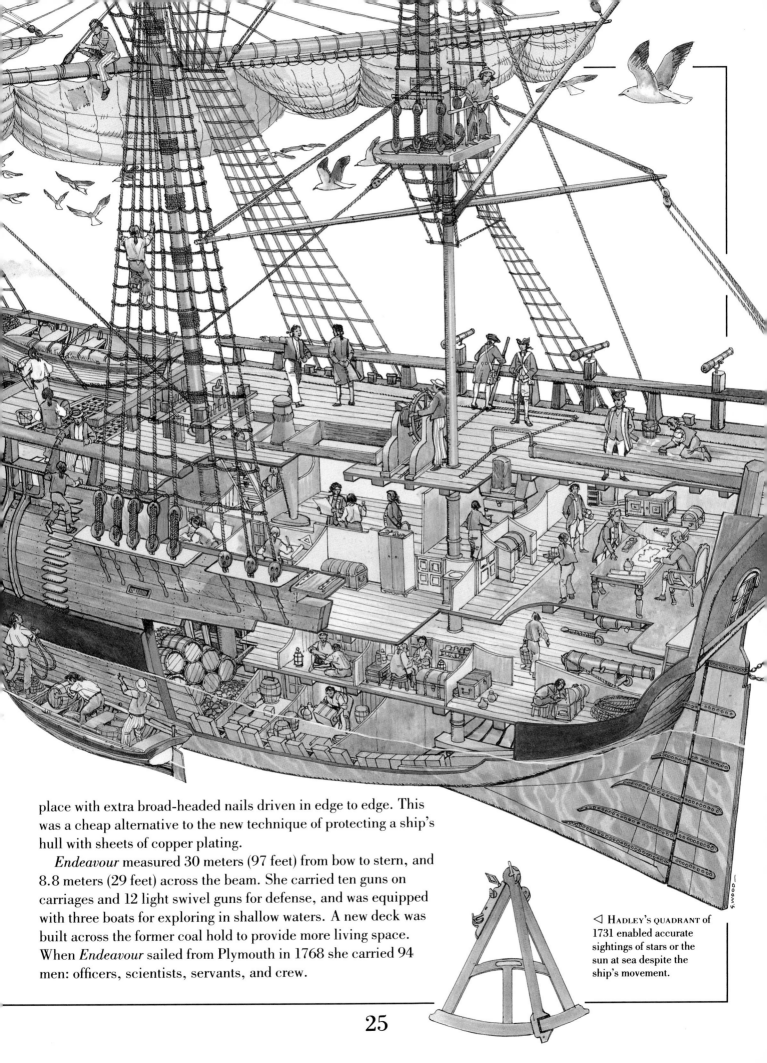

place with extra broad-headed nails driven in edge to edge. This was a cheap alternative to the new technique of protecting a ship's hull with sheets of copper plating.

Endeavour measured 30 meters (97 feet) from bow to stern, and 8.8 meters (29 feet) across the beam. She carried ten guns on carriages and 12 light swivel guns for defense, and was equipped with three boats for exploring in shallow waters. A new deck was built across the former coal hold to provide more living space. When *Endeavour* sailed from Plymouth in 1768 she carried 94 men: officers, scientists, servants, and crew.

◁ HADLEY'S QUADRANT of 1731 enabled accurate sightings of stars or the sun at sea despite the ship's movement.

SAIL VERSUS STEAM

△ A VERY EARLY STEAM paddlewheel tug, patented in 1736, shown towing a warship.

▽ CHARLOTTE DUNDAS (1802) was the first successful working steamer.

A FTER SEVERAL EXPERIMENTS with fitting steam engines in boats, the first steamboats appeared between 1800 and 1815. Driven by paddlewheels. they were used for towing barges on rivers and canals, and also as harbor tugs.

The first Atlantic crossing by a sailing ship fitted with a small steam engine was made (mostly under sail) by *Savannah* in 1819. It took until 1838 before *Sirius* made the first steam Atlantic crossing without the aid of sail. Unhampered by side paddles, fast sailing ships known as "clippers" kept the trade on most sea routes until the late 1850s. By the 1860s bigger, faster steamers, driven by the far more efficient stern screw, were threatening the sail clippers even on the long China tea and Australian wool routes. The opening of the Suez Canal in 1869 ended the need for fast voyages around Africa.

▽ THE TEA CLIPPER routes from Foochow, China, to London:

: 25,744 kilometers (16,000 miles), with a bonus of £100 for the first captain home and 10s a ton extra on his tea cargo.

▽ THE MOST FAMOUS TEA CLIPPER race of all time. On May 30, 1866 *Ariel*, *Taeping*, and *Serica* left Foochow on the same tide. After racing in sight of each other nearly all the

way, all three reached the Thames on September 6, on the same tide, after 99 days, and docked in London within two hours of each other. Their record was never beaten.

NORTH AMERICA

ASIA

ATLANTIC OCEAN

INDIAN OCEAN

AFRICA

SOUTH AMERICA

▽ PACKED with chests of the year's first tea crop, *Ariel* and *Taeping* race in company.

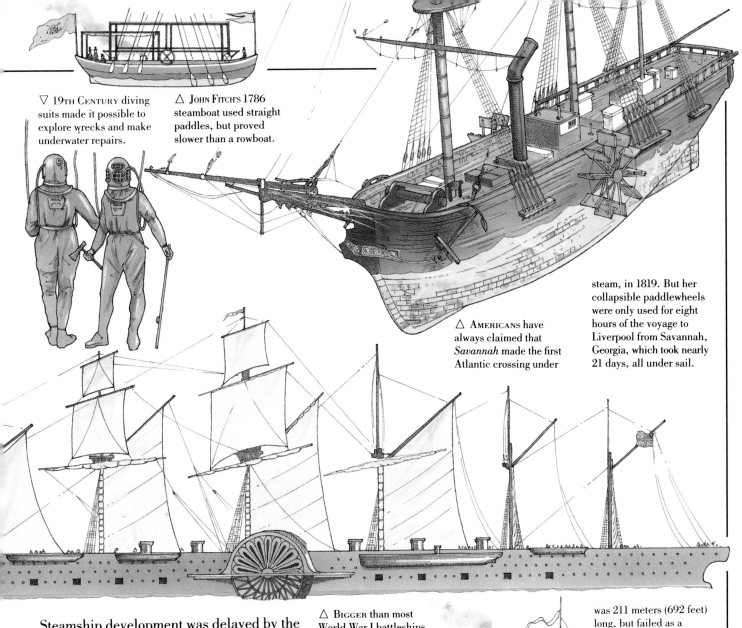

△ JOHN FITCH'S 1786 steamboat used straight paddles, but proved slower than a rowboat.

▽ 19TH CENTURY diving suits made it possible to explore wrecks and make underwater repairs.

△ AMERICANS have always claimed that *Savannah* made the first Atlantic crossing under steam, in 1819. But her collapsible paddlewheels were only used for eight hours of the voyage to Liverpool from Savannah, Georgia, which took nearly 21 days, all under sail.

Steamship development was delayed by the long struggle between paddlewheel and screw. The first screw-driven iron steamer to cross the Atlantic was I.K. Brunel's *Great Britain* in 1845, but she still carried a full sail rig. So did what was then the world's biggest ship, Brunel's 27,400-ton *Great Eastern* (1858). Driven by side paddles and a stern screw, *Great Eastern* also carried six masts.

During these years of mounting competition, sail clippers like the lovely *Cutty Sark* reached their peak of excellence. But they could only sail faster than steamships with the right wind. By the 1880s, steamers offered not only much bigger cargoes than the slim clippers could carry, but far more regularity of service in all weathers. Clippers were simply unable to compete.

△ BIGGER than most World War I battleships, the *Great Eastern* (1858) was 211 meters (692 feet) long, but failed as a passenger-carrier.

△ STEAM POWER OPENED the great rivers of Europe to regular passenger and freight traffic. This is the Rhine steamer *Friedrich Wilhelm*, shown carrying a passenger coach.

▽ AUXILIARY SAILS WERE used for many years on the River Seine. This French river steamer, which operated between Le Havre and Rouen, carried sails on three masts as well as a paddlewheel.

BATTLESHIPS

△ FRANCE'S *Gloire* (1859) was the first ironclad. She was a wooden steam frigate with a broadside of 60 guns. Her sides were protected by a belt of iron plates 11 centimeters (4.5 inches) thick.

T HE DEVELOPMENT OF THE MODERN BATTLESHIP was boosted by the coming of steam power, iron construction, and the use of explosive shells instead of iron shot. By the late 1850s warships were being built with strips or "belts" of armour plate along the waterline. The first of these were France's *Gloire* (1859) and Britain's all-iron *Warrior* (1860). Though seagoing "ironclads" needed masts and sails for long voyages, coastal and river ironclads did not.

The American Civil War (1861-65) saw the first battle between ironclads (*Merrimack* and *Monitor*, on March 9, 1862). Their armor saved them from damage even at point-blank range.

◁△ THE FIRST FIGHT between ironclads: *Merrimack* and *Monitor* fight at point-blank range during the American Civil War.

▷ △ BRITAIN'S *DREADNOUGHT* of 1906, showing her "all big-gun" armament of five twin 12-inch gun turrets designed for all-around fire.

◁ THE FIRST WARSHIP built completely of iron, *Warrior* (1860) was designed to out-class France's *Gloire*.

△ *MERRIMACK* (1862) was built up from the hull of a frigate, topped with an armored shield.

▷ GERMANY'S *BISMARCK* was the world's most powerful battleship when launched in 1939. She was armed with eight 38-centimeter (15-inch) guns and was sunk after an epic sea battle on May 27, 1941.

The 30 years after the American Civil War transformed the battleship. More powerful engines did away with the need for masts and sails; guns in moving turrets replaced the traditional broadsides; cordite explosive and rifled, breech-loading guns replaced the old muzzle-loading smoothbore guns.

The guns of Britain's *Dreadnought* (1906) fired shells measuring 30.4 centimeters (12 inches) across. The biggest battleships ever built were Japan's *Yamato* and *Musashi* (1940), both sunk in World War II. Armed with nine 45.9-centimeter (18-inch) guns, they displaced 71,659 tons at full load – 50,959 tons more than *Dreadnought*, and 83.5 meters (274 feet) longer.

▷ BRITAIN'S *Warspite* (1914) belonged to the first class of battleships designed to replace coal with oil fuel.

△ UNDERWATER "bulges" gave protection against torpedoes.

▽ SWORDFISH aircraft attacked *Bismarck*.

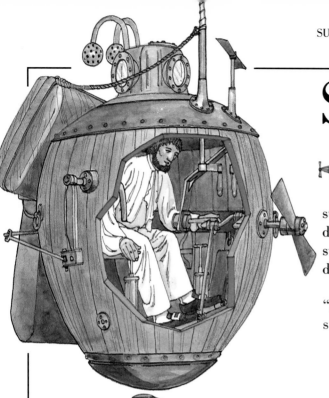

SUBMARINES

DAVID BUSHNELL'S *TURTLE* (*left*) of 1776 was the first submersible craft to attack a surface warship. This water-tight wooden egg was an American design. It had tanks which could be pumped full of water to submerge the craft just below water level, hand-driven screws to drive it up, down, and forward.

Also muscle-powered, though some had steam engines, the "Davids" (*below*) of the American Civil War (1861–65) were larger submersibles with metal hulls, carrying an explosive charge.

◁ THE *HUNLEY*, a hand-driven "David" of the American Civil War, was the first submersible to sink a surface warship: U.S.S. *Housatonic*, on February 17th, 1864. But the blast of the spar torpedo sank *Hunley* as well, drowning all nine of her crew.

▷ SHIPPED to warn the crew of bad air, caged mice were often spoiled pets on board!

▽ THE FIRST POWERED SUBMERSIBLE with an air-breathing gasoline engine for surface use and an electric motor for submerged propulsion was the American *Holland* of 1900. Displacing 107 tons, the "Holland" type carried a crew of seven.

△ THE PERISCOPE, for seeing above the surface when submerged, was an improvement over the dome with porthole.

The "Hollands" of the 1890s (*above*) used the new inventions of the internal combustion engine and self-propelled torpedoes fired from under water through airtight tubes.

△ IN THE "HOLLANDS," there was only room for a single bow torpedo tube.

▷ PRESSURE-PUMPED LAVATORY for use when submerged.

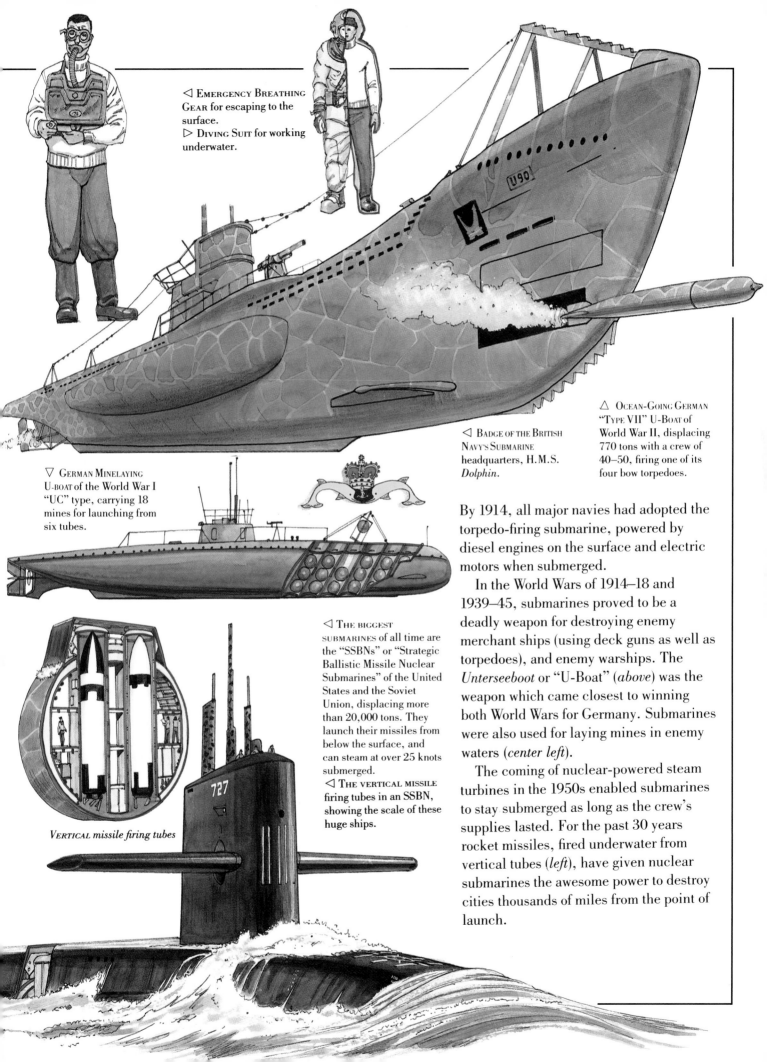

◁ EMERGENCY BREATHING GEAR for escaping to the surface.
▷ DIVING SUIT for working underwater.

△ OCEAN-GOING GERMAN "TYPE VII" U-BOAT of World War II, displacing 770 tons with a crew of 40–50, firing one of its four bow torpedoes.

▽ GERMAN MINELAYING U-BOAT of the World War I "UC" type, carrying 18 mines for launching from six tubes.

◁ BADGE OF THE BRITISH NAVY'S SUBMARINE headquarters, H.M.S. Dolphin.

◁ THE BIGGEST SUBMARINES of all time are the "SSBNs" or "Strategic Ballistic Missile Nuclear Submarines" of the United States and the Soviet Union, displacing more than 20,000 tons. They launch their missiles from below the surface, and can steam at over 25 knots submerged.
◁ THE VERTICAL MISSILE firing tubes in an SSBN, showing the scale of these huge ships.

Vertical missile firing tubes

By 1914, all major navies had adopted the torpedo-firing submarine, powered by diesel engines on the surface and electric motors when submerged.

In the World Wars of 1914–18 and 1939–45, submarines proved to be a deadly weapon for destroying enemy merchant ships (using deck guns as well as torpedoes), and enemy warships. The *Unterseeboot* or "U-Boat" (*above*) was the weapon which came closest to winning both World Wars for Germany. Submarines were also used for laying mines in enemy waters (*center left*).

The coming of nuclear-powered steam turbines in the 1950s enabled submarines to stay submerged as long as the crew's supplies lasted. For the past 30 years rocket missiles, fired underwater from vertical tubes (*left*), have given nuclear submarines the awesome power to destroy cities thousands of miles from the point of launch.

TITANIC

THE *TITANIC* STORY remains an enduring tragedy of the sea. The biggest, most beautiful, most luxurious passenger liner afloat, *Titanic* was fitted with safety features supposed to make her unsinkable – yet she was sunk on her very first voyage by an iceberg, with dreadful loss of life. The new aid of radio distress messages enabled 705 survivors to be picked up, but 1,522 men, women, and children died in the disaster.

Titanic and her two sister-ships, *Olympic* and *Britannic*, were ordered in 1908 to win the Atlantic luxury passenger trade for the White Star Line. When complete in March 1912, *Titanic*'s extra luxury features made her the world's biggest ship, at 52,250 tons.

△ *TITANIC* at sea: the biggest, most beautiful and luxurious ship ever built, confidently believed to be unsinkable.

▽ FOR OVER 70 YEARS IT was hoped that *Titanic* would someday be found to have sunk intact. But

when found in 1985 it was discovered that during her plunge she had broken in half between her third and fourth funnels.

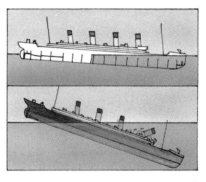

Titanic measured 268.8 meters (882 feet) long by 28 meters (92 feet) across the beam, and 92 feet from keel to Boat Deck. Her "water-tight" bulkheads divided the ship into 15 compartments but did not run the full depth of the ship. If more than four compartments were flooded, as happened on the night of April 14–15, 1912, water

overflowed one by one into the other compartments until the ship sank. And there was only lifeboat capacity for 1,178, meaning that even if all boats left full – which they did not – over 1,000 people would still be left aboard. Ever since the *Titanic* disaster, the rule has been "lifeboats for everyone."

When *Titanic*'s wreck was found and explored by camera, many mysteries about her sinking were solved, but one remained: the damage done by the iceberg. *Titanic*'s 137-meter (450-foot) bow section had plowed deep into the seabed, burying the plates on the forward starboard hull, which the iceberg had slashed open.

▽ DESPITE WARNINGS OF ice, *Titanic* was not re-routed far enough south to avoid it. When an iceberg was sighted, *Titanic* swung to port, but not enough to escape a slicing collision down her side.

▽ IF *TITANIC* HAD HIT the iceberg head-on, probably crumpling no more than her first three compartments, she would most likely have remained afloat.

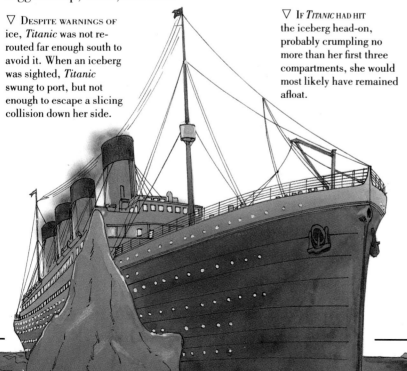

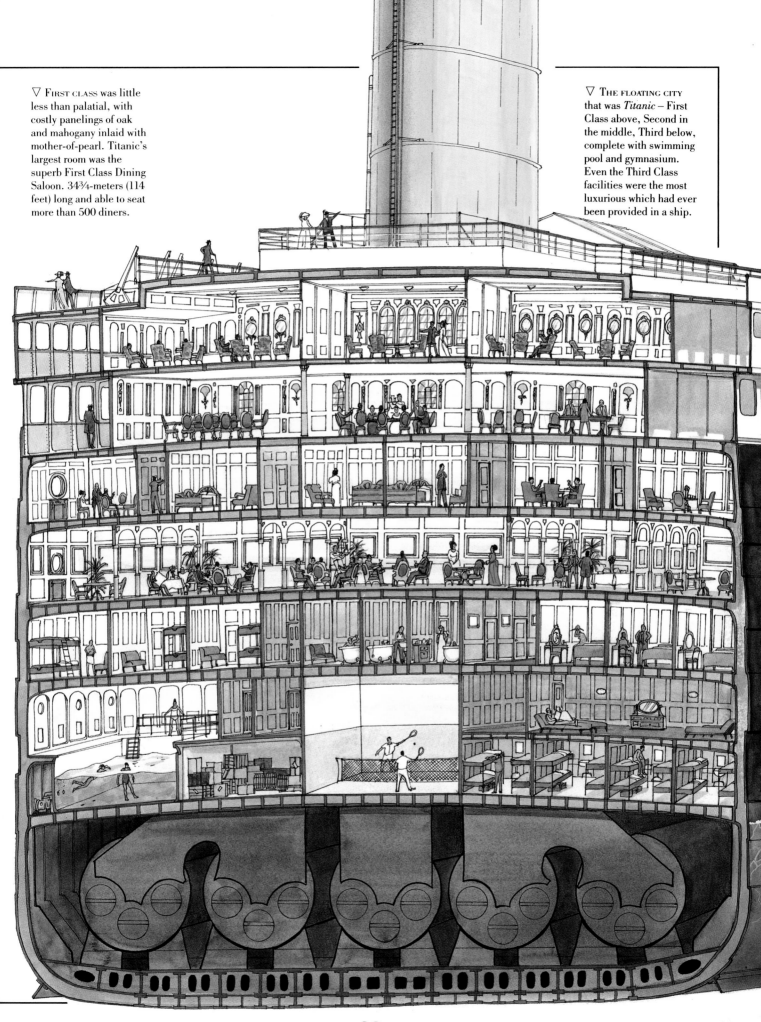

▽ First class was little less than palatial, with costly panelings of oak and mahogany inlaid with mother-of-pearl. Titanic's largest room was the superb First Class Dining Saloon. 34¾-meters (114 feet) long and able to seat more than 500 diners.

▽ The floating city that was *Titanic* – First Class above, Second in the middle, Third below, complete with swimming pool and gymnasium. Even the Third Class facilities were the most luxurious which had ever been provided in a ship.

33

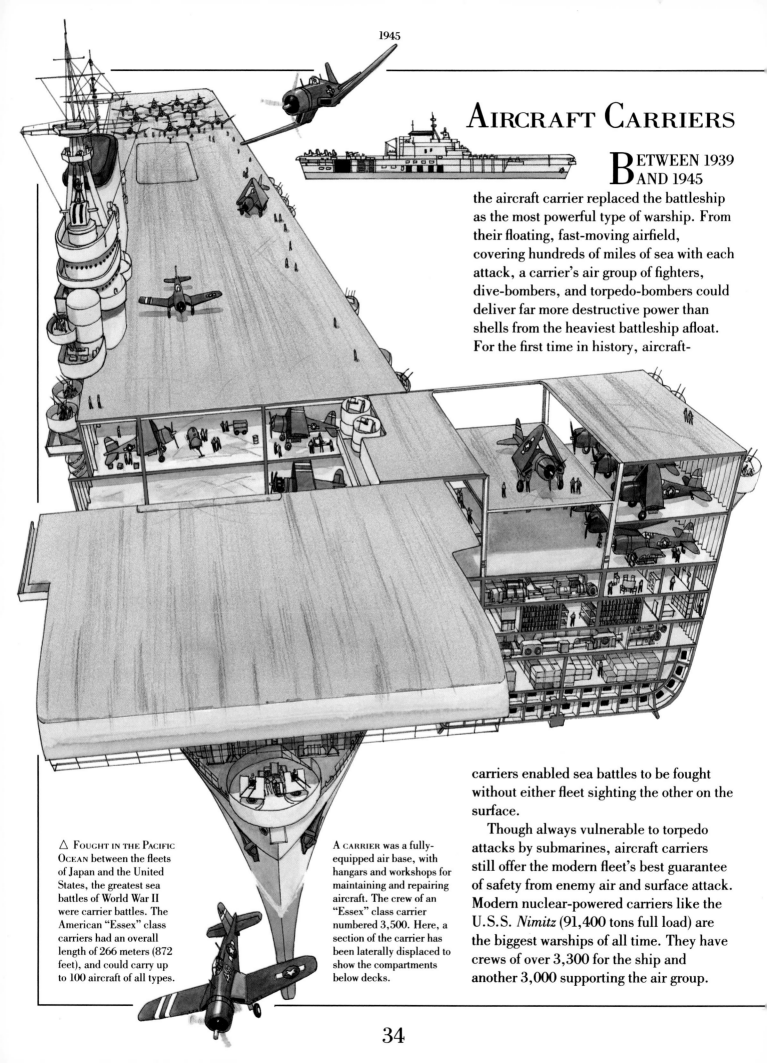

AIRCRAFT CARRIERS

BETWEEN 1939 **AND** 1945

1945

the aircraft carrier replaced the battleship as the most powerful type of warship. From their floating, fast-moving airfield, covering hundreds of miles of sea with each attack, a carrier's air group of fighters, dive-bombers, and torpedo-bombers could deliver far more destructive power than shells from the heaviest battleship afloat. For the first time in history, aircraft-

carriers enabled sea battles to be fought without either fleet sighting the other on the surface.

Though always vulnerable to torpedo attacks by submarines, aircraft carriers still offer the modern fleet's best guarantee of safety from enemy air and surface attack. Modern nuclear-powered carriers like the U.S.S. *Nimitz* (91,400 tons full load) are the biggest warships of all time. They have crews of over 3,300 for the ship and another 3,000 supporting the air group.

△ FOUGHT IN THE PACIFIC OCEAN between the fleets of Japan and the United States, the greatest sea battles of World War II were carrier battles. The American "Essex" class carriers had an overall length of 266 meters (872 feet), and could carry up to 100 aircraft of all types.

A CARRIER was a fully-equipped air base, with hangars and workshops for maintaining and repairing aircraft. The crew of an "Essex" class carrier numbered 3,500. Here, a section of the carrier has been laterally displaced to show the compartments below decks.

GUIDED-MISSILE WARSHIPS

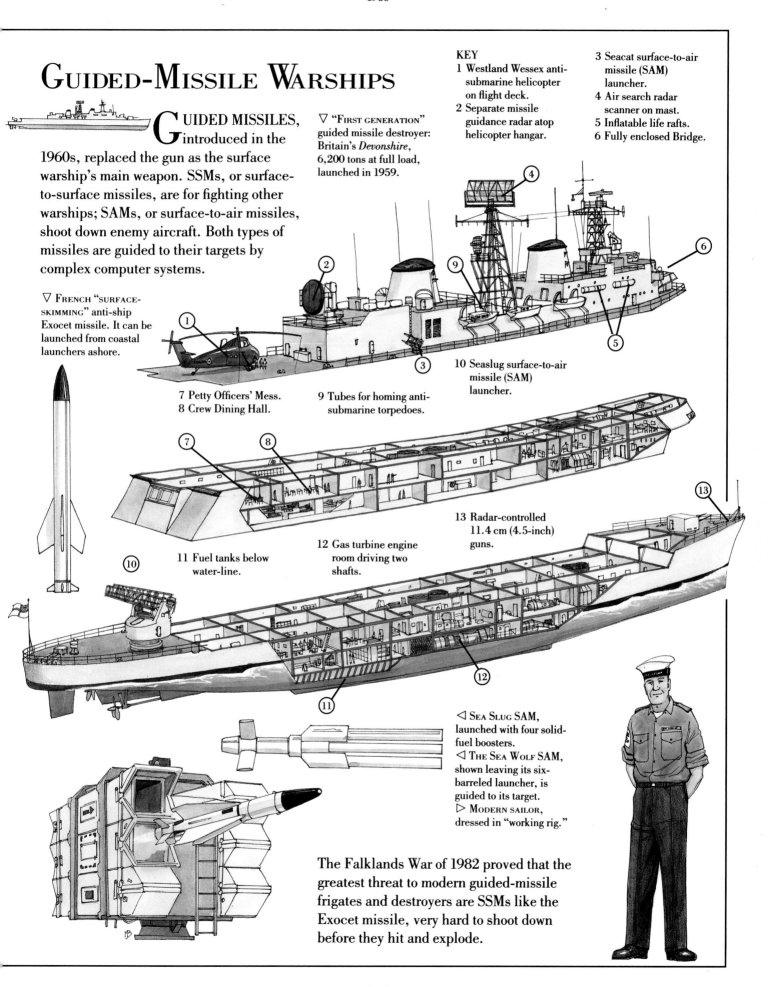

GUIDED MISSILES, introduced in the 1960s, replaced the gun as the surface warship's main weapon. SSMs, or surface-to-surface missiles, are for fighting other warships; SAMs, or surface-to-air missiles, shoot down enemy aircraft. Both types of missiles are guided to their targets by complex computer systems.

▽ FRENCH "SURFACE-SKIMMING" anti-ship Exocet missile. It can be launched from coastal launchers ashore.

▽ "FIRST GENERATION" guided missile destroyer: Britain's *Devonshire*, 6,200 tons at full load, launched in 1959.

KEY
1 Westland Wessex anti-submarine helicopter on flight deck.
2 Separate missile guidance radar atop helicopter hangar.
3 Seacat surface-to-air missile (SAM) launcher.
4 Air search radar scanner on mast.
5 Inflatable life rafts.
6 Fully enclosed Bridge.

7 Petty Officers' Mess.
8 Crew Dining Hall.

9 Tubes for homing anti-submarine torpedoes.

10 Seaslug surface-to-air missile (SAM) launcher.

11 Fuel tanks below water-line.

12 Gas turbine engine room driving two shafts.

13 Radar-controlled 11.4 cm (4.5-inch) guns.

◁ SEA SLUG SAM, launched with four solid-fuel boosters.
◁ THE SEA WOLF SAM, shown leaving its six-barreled launcher, is guided to its target.
▷ MODERN SAILOR, dressed in "working rig."

The Falklands War of 1982 proved that the greatest threat to modern guided-missile frigates and destroyers are SSMs like the Exocet missile, very hard to shoot down before they hit and explode.

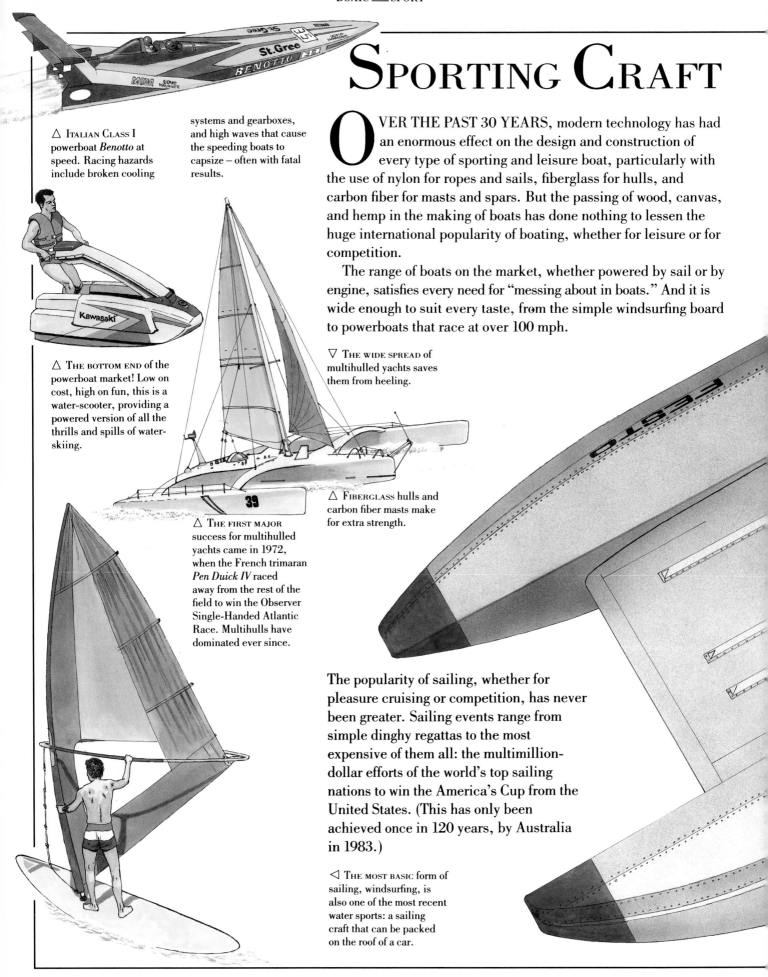

SPORTING CRAFT

OVER THE PAST 30 YEARS, modern technology has had an enormous effect on the design and construction of every type of sporting and leisure boat, particularly with the use of nylon for ropes and sails, fiberglass for hulls, and carbon fiber for masts and spars. But the passing of wood, canvas, and hemp in the making of boats has done nothing to lessen the huge international popularity of boating, whether for leisure or for competition.

The range of boats on the market, whether powered by sail or by engine, satisfies every need for "messing about in boats." And it is wide enough to suit every taste, from the simple windsurfing board to powerboats that race at over 100 mph.

△ ITALIAN CLASS I powerboat *Benotto* at speed. Racing hazards include broken cooling systems and gearboxes, and high waves that cause the speeding boats to capsize – often with fatal results.

△ THE BOTTOM END of the powerboat market! Low on cost, high on fun, this is a water-scooter, providing a powered version of all the thrills and spills of water-skiing.

▽ THE WIDE SPREAD of multihulled yachts saves them from heeling.

△ THE FIRST MAJOR success for multihulled yachts came in 1972, when the French trimaran *Pen Duick IV* raced away from the rest of the field to win the Observer Single-Handed Atlantic Race. Multihulls have dominated ever since.

△ FIBERGLASS hulls and carbon fiber masts make for extra strength.

The popularity of sailing, whether for pleasure cruising or competition, has never been greater. Sailing events range from simple dinghy regattas to the most expensive of them all: the multimillion-dollar efforts of the world's top sailing nations to win the America's Cup from the United States. (This has only been achieved once in 120 years, by Australia in 1983.)

◁ THE MOST BASIC form of sailing, windsurfing, is also one of the most recent water sports: a sailing craft that can be packed on the roof of a car.

△ YACHT RACE UNDER WAY. The most thrilling races are those fought out when there is hardly any wind, taking sailors' skills to the utmost.

△ ITALIAN CLASS I catamaran powerboat *Bagutta*. These boats travel so fast, the crewmen have to be strapped into their cockpits like fighter pilots.

Perhaps the most exciting form of competitive boating is high-speed powerboat racing. As with sailing, in recent years this has developed into a duel between single-hulled boats and more stable catamarans. Both types have immensely powerful engines of 1,500 horsepower or more, yielding speeds of more than 100 mph. It is common for boats in a long race to keep up this average speed from start to finish. The cost of producing these splendid but often highly dangerous racers is so high that, as in Formula 1 car racing, it requires cash sponsorship from big business.

HOVERCRAFT

△ *SeaCat*, designed to carry 80 cars and 450 passengers. *SeaCat* is 74 meters (243 feet) long and 26 meters (85 feet) wide.

The design of its catamaran hull is shaped to produce a hydrofoil lifting effect, cruising at 35 knots.

THE SEARCH FOR SPEED AND EFFICIENCY

prompted two useful new types of passenger ferry, in the form of the Hovercraft and the hydrofoil. The Hovercraft rides on a trapped cushion of air created by a downward-pointing fan, and is driven forward by propellers. It can travel over land and water, and has proved of great value ferrying passengers across seaways such as the English Channel. Hydrofoils, used for longer sea crossings, raise the hull of the boat from the water on a rigid water-ski framework, when the boat is traveling at great speed. Hydrofoils travel faster than Hovercraft.

△ THE FIRST HOVERCRAFT: SR-N1 (1959), powered by a 450 horsepower engine.

△ THE FIRST successful hydrofoil (1906) was driven by air propellers.

▽ SHIP OR AIRCRAFT? The Hovercraft can ride over land or water, gliding on the cushion of air trapped inside its "skirt."

△ HYDROFOIL: a conventional hull on a winglike framework.

△ HOVERCRAFT: a surface-skimmer that can cruise from sea to beach.

Though completely different craft, both types ride safely on the water in the event of power failure. The hydrofoil cruises on its conventionally-shaped hull when moving at low speeds.

▷ *SEACAT* PASSENGERS will relax on the big observation deck during the 2 hour 40 minute Channel crossing from Portsmouth to Cherbourg.

△ FOR CRUISING the Swiss lakes: PT-150-DC hydrofoil, able to carry 250 passengers at 67.5 kph (42 mph).

▽ CROSS-CHANNEL VT1 (B) Hovercraft (1969) carried 10 cars and 146 passengers.

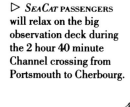

△ DRAWING MORE on hydrofoil rather than Hovercraft experience, *SeaCat's* twin hull is a

streamlined wave-slicer, designed to beat the often rough and choppy seas of the English Channel.

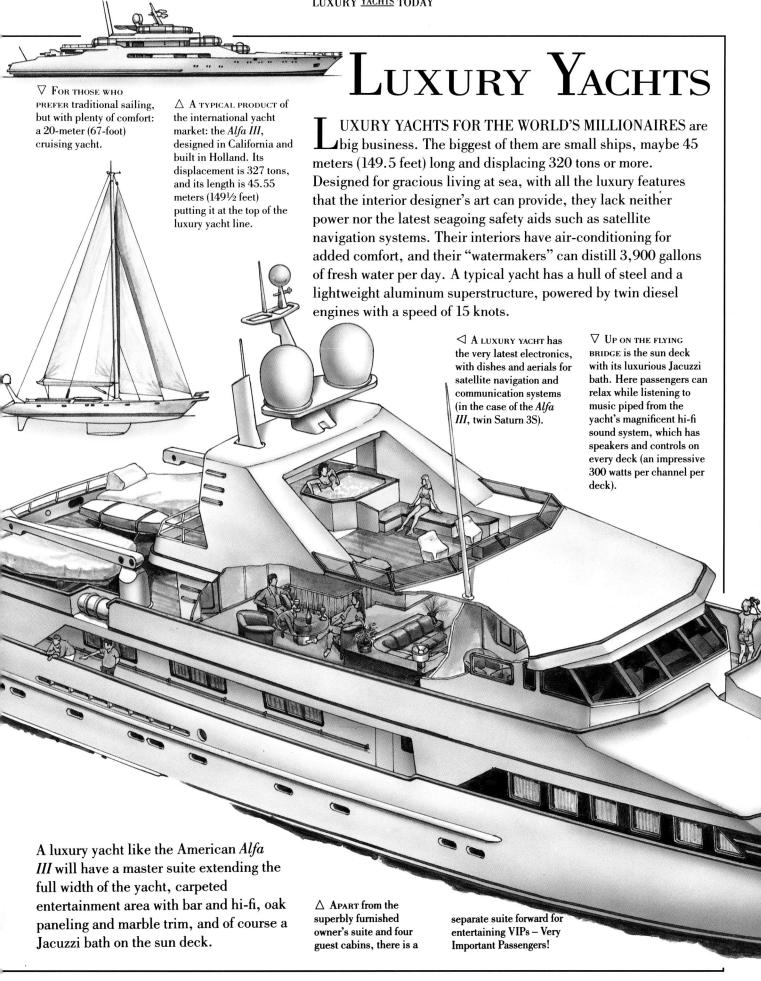

▽ FOR THOSE WHO PREFER traditional sailing, but with plenty of comfort: a 20-meter (67-foot) cruising yacht.

△ A TYPICAL PRODUCT of the international yacht market: the *Alfa III*, designed in California and built in Holland. Its displacement is 327 tons, and its length is 45.55 meters (149½ feet) putting it at the top of the luxury yacht line.

LUXURY YACHTS

LUXURY YACHTS FOR THE WORLD'S MILLIONAIRES are big business. The biggest of them are small ships, maybe 45 meters (149.5 feet) long and displacing 320 tons or more. Designed for gracious living at sea, with all the luxury features that the interior designer's art can provide, they lack neither power nor the latest seagoing safety aids such as satellite navigation systems. Their interiors have air-conditioning for added comfort, and their "watermakers" can distill 3,900 gallons of fresh water per day. A typical yacht has a hull of steel and a lightweight aluminum superstructure, powered by twin diesel engines with a speed of 15 knots.

◁ A LUXURY YACHT has the very latest electronics, with dishes and aerials for satellite navigation and communication systems (in the case of the *Alfa III*, twin Saturn 3S).

▽ UP ON THE FLYING BRIDGE is the sun deck with its luxurious Jacuzzi bath. Here passengers can relax while listening to music piped from the yacht's magnificent hi-fi sound system, which has speakers and controls on every deck (an impressive 300 watts per channel per deck).

A luxury yacht like the American *Alfa III* will have a master suite extending the full width of the yacht, carpeted entertainment area with bar and hi-fi, oak paneling and marble trim, and of course a Jacuzzi bath on the sun deck.

△ APART from the superbly furnished owner's suite and four guest cabins, there is a separate suite forward for entertaining VIPs – Very Important Passengers!

OIL TANKERS

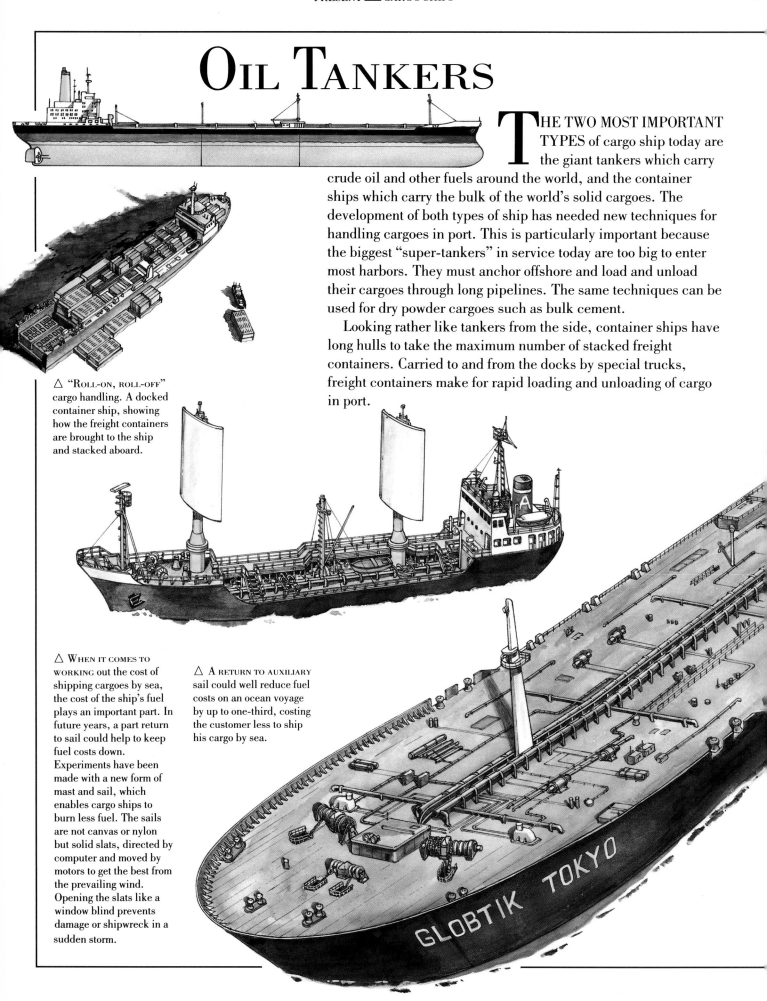

THE TWO MOST IMPORTANT TYPES of cargo ship today are the giant tankers which carry crude oil and other fuels around the world, and the container ships which carry the bulk of the world's solid cargoes. The development of both types of ship has needed new techniques for handling cargoes in port. This is particularly important because the biggest "super-tankers" in service today are too big to enter most harbors. They must anchor offshore and load and unload their cargoes through long pipelines. The same techniques can be used for dry powder cargoes such as bulk cement.

Looking rather like tankers from the side, container ships have long hulls to take the maximum number of stacked freight containers. Carried to and from the docks by special trucks, freight containers make for rapid loading and unloading of cargo in port.

△ "ROLL-ON, ROLL-OFF" cargo handling. A docked container ship, showing how the freight containers are brought to the ship and stacked aboard.

△ WHEN IT COMES TO WORKING OUT the cost of shipping cargoes by sea, the cost of the ship's fuel plays an important part. In future years, a part return to sail could help to keep fuel costs down. Experiments have been made with a new form of mast and sail, which enables cargo ships to burn less fuel. The sails are not canvas or nylon but solid slats, directed by computer and moved by motors to get the best from the prevailing wind. Opening the slats like a window blind prevents damage or shipwreck in a sudden storm.

△ A RETURN TO AUXILIARY sail could well reduce fuel costs on an ocean voyage by up to one-third, costing the customer less to ship his cargo by sea.

GLOBTIK TOKYO

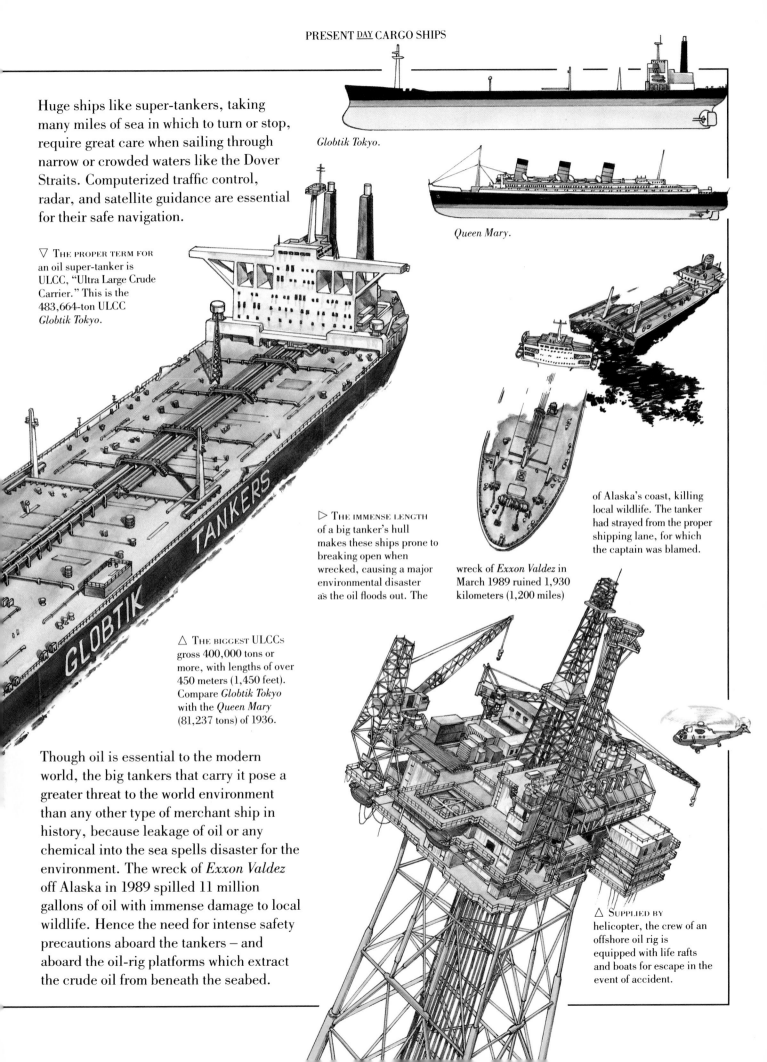

Huge ships like super-tankers, taking many miles of sea in which to turn or stop, require great care when sailing through narrow or crowded waters like the Dover Straits. Computerized traffic control, radar, and satellite guidance are essential for their safe navigation.

Globtik Tokyo.

Queen Mary.

▽ THE PROPER TERM FOR an oil super-tanker is ULCC, "Ultra Large Crude Carrier." This is the 483,664-ton ULCC *Globtik Tokyo.*

▷ THE IMMENSE LENGTH of a big tanker's hull makes these ships prone to breaking open when wrecked, causing a major environmental disaster as the oil floods out. The

wreck of *Exxon Valdez* in March 1989 ruined 1,930 kilometers (1,200 miles)

of Alaska's coast, killing local wildlife. The tanker had strayed from the proper shipping lane, for which the captain was blamed.

△ THE BIGGEST ULCCs gross 400,000 tons or more, with lengths of over 450 meters (1,450 feet). Compare *Globtik Tokyo* with the *Queen Mary* (81,237 tons) of 1936.

Though oil is essential to the modern world, the big tankers that carry it pose a greater threat to the world environment than any other type of merchant ship in history, because leakage of oil or any chemical into the sea spells disaster for the environment. The wreck of *Exxon Valdez* off Alaska in 1989 spilled 11 million gallons of oil with immense damage to local wildlife. Hence the need for intense safety precautions aboard the tankers – and aboard the oil-rig platforms which extract the crude oil from beneath the seabed.

△ SUPPLIED BY helicopter, the crew of an offshore oil rig is equipped with life rafts and boats for escape in the event of accident.

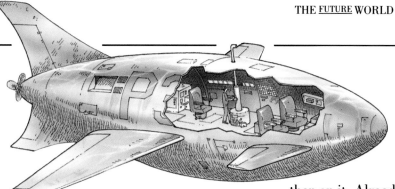

THE FUTURE

△ ONE IDEA for the design of future submarines is to borrow the principles of flight used by aircraft. Today's submarines are still floating ships which use flooding ballast tanks to submerge and surface. But the "flying submarine" idea would only use small tanks to float on the surface in port. At sea it would use aircraftlike wings to provide lift, with moving controls for turning, diving, and climbing. The hull of the "flying submarine" would be much stronger and thicker, enabling it to dive far deeper than today's submarines.

LOOKING TO THE FUTURE, the chances are that there will be far more activity below the surface than on it. Already submarines with nuclear power, freed from the effects of wind, weather, and waves, can steam at up to 40 knots. Big cargo-carrying submarines, able to achieve speeds previously possible only with luxury surface liners, could transform the cost of delivering freight by sea. Submarines fitted with viewing lounges could offer vacationers wonderful underwater wildlife safaris, but if pollution of the seas continues at its present rate, there may be little left to see.

The shallow waters of the world's continental shelves are already providing new sources of energy such as oil and gas. But they will almost certainly be used more and more to gather food from the sea to feed the ever-growing population of the world.

Experiments have already shown that colonies on the seabed, manned by divers, can be used to conserve fish stocks for controlled "harvesting." For such colonies in the future, small submarines would certainly be used to bring crews and supplies to and from the surface. These submarines would dock with the undersea buildings, just as space shuttles dock with orbiting space stations. Loading and unloading would be carried out by means of airlocks. Each station would have its own small submarine for patrolling and exploring the seabed.

△ TODAY'S BIGGEST SUBMARINES are the huge warships designed to carry nuclear missiles. But in the future these deadly ships could well be used for carrying cargoes, passengers, or both. Such a submarine could carry passengers on an "undersea wildlife safari."

▽ UNDERSEA COLONY on the seabed, manned by a crew of expert divers living in comfortable quarters when not at work outside.

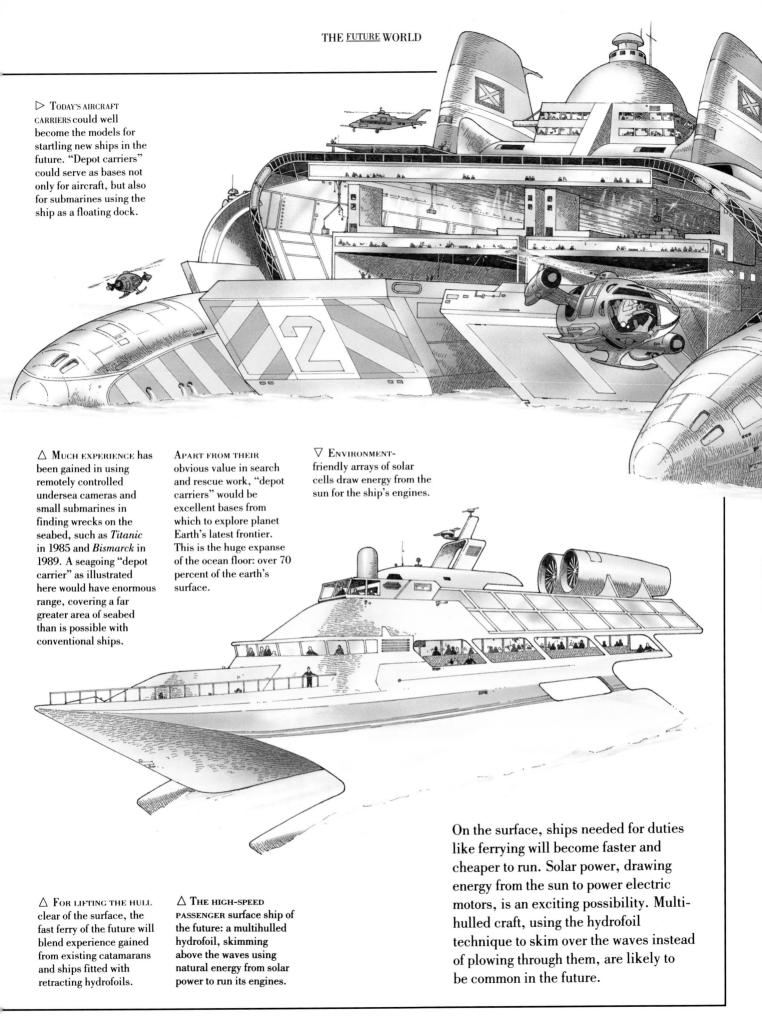

▷ TODAY'S AIRCRAFT CARRIERS could well become the models for startling new ships in the future. "Depot carriers" could serve as bases not only for aircraft, but also for submarines using the ship as a floating dock.

△ MUCH EXPERIENCE has been gained in using remotely controlled undersea cameras and small submarines in finding wrecks on the seabed, such as *Titanic* in 1985 and *Bismarck* in 1989. A seagoing "depot carrier" as illustrated here would have enormous range, covering a far greater area of seabed than is possible with conventional ships.

APART FROM THEIR obvious value in search and rescue work, "depot carriers" would be excellent bases from which to explore planet Earth's latest frontier. This is the huge expanse of the ocean floor: over 70 percent of the earth's surface.

▽ ENVIRONMENT-friendly arrays of solar cells draw energy from the sun for the ship's engines.

△ FOR LIFTING THE HULL clear of the surface, the fast ferry of the future will blend experience gained from existing catamarans and ships fitted with retracting hydrofoils.

△ THE HIGH-SPEED PASSENGER surface ship of the future: a multihulled hydrofoil, skimming above the waves using natural energy from solar power to run its engines.

On the surface, ships needed for duties like ferrying will become faster and cheaper to run. Solar power, drawing energy from the sun to power electric motors, is an exciting possibility. Multi-hulled craft, using the hydrofoil technique to skim over the waves instead of plowing through them, are likely to be common in the future.

TIMELINE

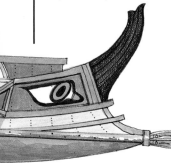

Egyptian cargo

B.C.
c.3400 First pictures of papyrus and wooden boats in Egypt.
c.2800 Seagoing Egyptian reed ships could have crossed Atlantic (proved by Thor Heyerdahl in *Ra I* and *Ra II*, 1969–70).

c.2560 Pharaoh Snofru of Egypt sends 40 ships to buy cedar wood for shipbuilding from Byblos in Syria.
c.2500 World's oldest wooden museum ship: the funeral barge of Pharaoh Khufu.
c.2500 Seagoing reed ships from Sumer (southern Iraq) could have reached India and Africa (proved by Thor Heyerdahl in *Tigris*, 1977).

Greek trireme

Viking coin

c.2400 First pictures of a war fleet: Pharaoh Sahure's 8-ship raid on the Syrian coast.
c.1500 Queen Hatshepsut's trading fleet sails from Egypt to "Punt" (probably Somaliland).
c.1180 First pictures of a sea battle depict Pharaoh Rameses III's defeat of the "Sea Peoples."
480 Battle of Salamis: Greek triremes (3-banked oared galleys) shatter Persian galley fleet.
264–241 Naval war between Rome and Carthage: Roman galley fleet victories at Mylae (260), Ecnomus (256) and Aegatian Islands (241).
31 Battle of Actium: fleet of Octavius Caesar defeats heavy galleys of Mark Antony and Cleopatra.

A.D.
c.100–300 Roman merchant fleets sail regularly from Egypt to India.
c.350–500 Angles and Saxons invade Britain in open rowing longships.
c.500 Refugee Irish monks could have reached America in wicker-frame, leather-covered *currrachs* (proved by Tim Severin with *Brendan*, 1976).
875–985 Viking colonists in square-sail longships settle Iceland and Greenland.
c.1000 Arabs in lateen-sail dhows could have reached China from Arabia (proved by Tim Severin in *Sindbad*, 1980).
c.1000–1006 Reported Viking voyages by Leif Eriksson and Thorfinn Karlesfni from Greenland to "Vinland" (North America).
c.1100 Pre-Inca colonists from South America could have reached Pacific islands on fleets of balsa rafts

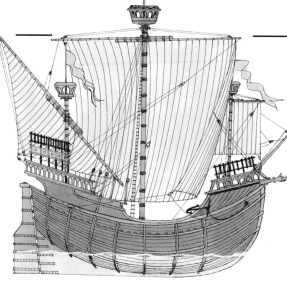

Medieval cog

(proved by Thor Heyerdahl with *Kon-Tiki*, 1947). Double-hulled canoe migrations spread population of Pacific islands from Hawaii to New Zealand (proved by Hawaiian-American *Hokule'a* project, 1976).
1150–1250 North European shipbuilders replace the steering oar with the stern rudder.
1290 Marco Polo of Venice describes large Chinese passenger-carrying merchant junks with four masts, 60 cabins, and watertight hull compartments.
c.1350–1450 The single-masted European clinker-built cog gives place to the three-masted,

Sailor c. 1450

carvel-built carrack.
c.1425–1485 Three-masted Portuguese caravels explore West African coast.
1488–89 Bartholomew Diaz of Portugal, with two caravels, finds sea route to India past Cape of Good Hope.
1492–1493 Christopher Columbus, with two caravels and a storeship, crosses the

Cook's Endeavour

Atlantic and claims the West Indies for Spain.
1493–1496 Second voyage of Columbus to West Indies.
1497 John Cabot, sailing from Bristol, England, discovers Newfoundland.
1498 Third voyage of Columbus discovers Trinidad and South America.
1498–1499 Vasco da Gama makes first voyage from Europe to India around Africa.
1502–1504 Fourth voyage of Columbus explores coast of Honduras and Panama.

1511–1512 Henry VIII of England builds his warships *Mary Rose* and *Great Harry*, with decks of cannon firing broadsides.
1513 Vasco Nuñez de Balboa sights Pacific Ocean from Panama Isthmus.
1519–1522 Ferdinand Magellan dies after first European crossing of the Pacific Ocean; his *Victoria* completes the first voyage around the world.
1545 *Mary Rose* sunk; raised 1982 and displayed at Portsmouth, England, as world's oldest museum sailing warship.
c.1560–1580 Broadside-firing galleon emerges as leading European warship type.
1571 Battle of Lepanto: last major sea fight between oared galley fleets.
1588 Spanish Armada defeated after first sea fights between broadside-firing fleets.
c.1610–1830 World's richest cargoes carried in armed merchant ships of European East India companies.
1620 *Mayflower* lands Pilgrims at Plymouth, Mass.; voyage re-enacted in 1957 by *Mayflower II*, a replica.
1628 Swedish 64-gun *Vasa* sunk; raised 1961 and preserved at Stockholm, Sweden, as world's only 17th century museum warship.
1765 H.M.S. *Victory* launched; preserved at Portsmouth, England, as world's only museum "First Rate" ship of the line.
1768–1771 James Cook, in the converted Whitby coal ship *Endeavour*, discovers New Zealand and maps east coast of Australia.
1772–1775 Cook's second voyage circles Antarctica.
1776 In America's Revolutionary War, David Bushnell's *Turtle* carries

Captain c. 1800

out first submersible attack on a surface warship.

1776–1779 Cook's third Pacific voyage discovers Hawaii, where he is killed.

1796 Launch of U.S.S. *Constitution* and *Constellation*; preserved at Boston and Baltimore as the world's only museum sailing frigates.

1802 Robert Fulton's submarine *Nautilus* is rejected by the French and British navies. In

Steamboat c. 1850

Scotland, *Charlotte Dundas* becomes the world's first working steamboat.

1819 *Savannah* crosses Atlantic under sail with help of small steam engine.

1827 Battle of Navarino: last sea battle between sailing fleets.

c. 1835 Steam tugs in general use in world's major ports.

1838 *Sirius* crosses Atlantic under steam with aid of sail. Brunel's *Great Western*, specially designed for the Atlantic

route, enters service.

1845 Tug of war between British steam sloops *Alecto* and *Rattler* proves superiority of screw propeller over paddlewheel. Brunel's all-iron *Great Britain* makes first Atlantic steam crossing under screw propulsion.

1854 Wooden Turkish fleet destroyed at Sinope by Russian fleet firing explosive shells.

1858 Launch of *Great Eastern* (paddlewheel/screw), the world's biggest ship at 27,400 tons.

1859 First ironclad warship: France's *Gloire*, with armor plate over wooden hull.

1860 Britain's broadside-firing *Warrior*, preserved at Portsmouth, England, as world's first all-iron warship with armor plate.

1862 First battle between ironclad warships (*Monitor* and *Merrimack*), featuring turret guns, in American Civil War.

1864 U.S.S. *Housatonic* becomes first warship sunk by a submersible (the Confederate *Hunley*).

1866 Battle of Lissa, first sea fight between fleets of steam ironclad rams. Epic China/London race between sailing tea clippers *Ariel*, *Taeping* and *Serica*.

1869 *Cutty Sark* built to capture declining sail clipper trade; preserved at Greenwich, London, as last of the tea clippers.

1877 First use of self-propelled explosive

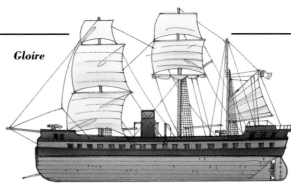

Gloire

torpedoes.

1891 Chilean battleship *Blanco Encalada* becomes first warship sunk by torpedoes.

1897 British *Turbinia*, world's first vessel powered by turbine engines (speed 30 knots).

1900 J. P. Holland's torpedo-firing submarine purchased by U.S. Navy; her design adopted for the submarine arms of the British, Japanese, and Russian navies.

1905 Battle of Tsushima: Japanese battleships shatter Russian fleet. Last "all-gun" sea battle, fought without intervention of submarines or aircraft.

1906 British "all big-gun" turbine-powered *Dreadnought* transforms battleship design and triggers "battleship building race" between Britain and Germany.

1911 Eugene Ely becomes the first aircraft pilot to land on and take off from a warship (cruiser U.S.S. *Pennsylvania*, fitted with a platform).

1912 *Titanic*, built as the world's biggest and most luxurious liner, is

Titanic

sunk by an iceberg with the loss of 1,522 lives.

1914 British cruisers *Aboukir*, *Hogue*, and *Cressy* sunk by single U-boat with loss of 1,459 men out of 2,200.

1915 Liner *Lusitania* sunk by U-boat with loss of 1,198 lives. British seaplanes off Dardanelles sink first ships with air-launched torpedoes.

1916 Battle of Jutland; last major engagement between battleship fleets.

1917 Unrestricted attacks by German U-boats come close to winning war for Germany, but are beaten by sailing merchant ships in convoy.

1918 On defeat of Germany, German battle fleet surrenders to Britain's Royal Navy.

1922 Washington Treaty seeks to limit size of future battleships by international agreement.

1923 World's first purpose-built aircraft carriers (Japanese *Hosho* and British *Hermes*) enter

service.

1940 Launch of Japan's *Yamato* and *Musashi*, the biggest battleships ever (71,659 tons, nine 18-inch guns). Italian battle fleet crippled at Taranto by British carrier-launched aircraft.

1941 Japanese carrier aircraft destroy American battle fleet at Pearl Harbor.

1942 Battle of the Coral Sea: first carrier-versus-carrier battle.

1943 Italian battleship *Roma* becomes first warship sunk by guided missile.

1945 World War II ends with aircraft carriers and attack submarines as

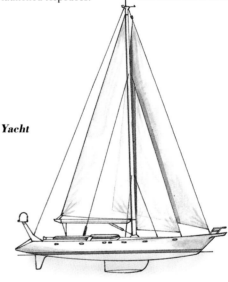

Yacht

dominant warship types.

1955 U.S.S. *Nautilus*, world's first nuclear-powered submarine.

1956 First commercial use of hydrofoil craft (Sicily-Italy ferries).

1968 SRN-4, commercial Hovercraft, enters service (English Channel ferries).

1982 Falklands War: first "missile war" at sea.

1991 American "Iowa" class battleships (launched 1943) bombard Iraqi targets with 16-inch shells and Tomahawk cruise missiles in Gulf War to liberate Kuwait.

GLOSSARY

Astrolabe Navigator's instrument for measuring the altitude, or height, of the sun and stars, to calculate the ship's latitude.

Belaying pins Heavy movable pins of wood or metal, placed in racks around a sailing ship for the quick securing of ropes.

Boatswain (pronounced bo'sun) Petty officer responsible for all work done on deck; in charge of sails, rigging, anchors, cables, and the like.

Bóum (Or *boom*) Two-masted, lateen-rigged Arab ship with hull of planks stitched and lashed together.

Bow The pointed foremost end of a ship.

Broadside Array of cannon placed to fire through ports cut in the side of a ship.

Bulkhead Vertical partition or wall dividing a ship into compartments.

Caravel Small trading ship of three or four masts, much used on early Spanish and Portuguese voyages of exploration from about 1420–1520.

Caravela latina Caravel rigged to carry lateen sails.

Caravela redonda Caravel rigged to carry square sails on mainmast and foremast.

Carrack Large trading ship of three or four masts of the late 14th and 15th centuries, blending the square rig of northern Europe with the lateen rig of the Mediterranean.

Carvel building Vessel built with outer planking laid flush, edge to edge.

Catamaran Sailing or powered vessel of two connected hulls.

Cathead Heavy timber projecting from a ship's bow for supporting an anchor.

Clinker building Vessel built with a shell of overlapping planks, braced inside.

Clipper American name for any sailing ship designed for very high speeds.

Cog Broad-beamed, clinker-built, single-masted North European trading ship of the 13th and 14th centuries.

Corvus (Latin for "crow") A heavy, spiked boarding bridge fitted in Roman warships to drop onto an enemy ship before boarding and capturing it.

Cuddy Cabin in the stern of a ship for the captain and his passengers; also a compartment where the officers had their meals.

Dhow General name for any Arab trading ship, most of them lateen-rigged sailing ships but some with engines.

Draft The depth of water taken up or "drawn" by a floating ship.

Flying bridge Bridge platform, raised above the deck.

Forecastle (pronounced "fo'c'sle") Once the raised fighting platform or "castle" in the bow of a medieval warship. Today it is the space beneath the foredeck, the crew's living quarters.

Frigate Once sailing warships with a single gundeck, not powerful enough to join the line of battle; today, specialized warships designed for hunting and destroying submarines.

Funnel Metal chimney to carry engine smoke and fumes clear of the deck.

Galleon (from Spanish *galeon*) Large 16th century trading ship, developed from the carrack but without a high-built forecastle.

Galley 1. Any oared fighting ship, and the world's oldest warship type (in service from the days of ancient Egypt to the coming of steam); 2. The cooking space or kitchen of a ship.

Hawsehole Opening in the ship's forward deck, right in the bows, through which the anchor cable or hawse passes.

Hull (from German *hülle*, "cloak," or "covering"). The main body and decks of a ship, excluding masts, funnels, and upperworks.

Ironclad Early name for wood or iron warships protected by armor plate.

Junk (From Portuguese *jonca*, Javanese *djong*) General name for Far Eastern sailing ships, especially Chinese or Javanese, with flat bottoms, high sterns and square bows, and matting sails stiffened with horizontal battens.

Keel The "backbone" of a ship.

Knot Measure of a ship's speed: 1 nautical mile (1,853 meters) per hour. From the measuring knots tied into a log line and streamed astern a ship, counting the knots that ran out to calculate the ship's speed.

Lateen Triangular sail of Arab and Mediterranean origin, enabling a ship to sail close to the wind.

Longship General name for Viking ships, clinker-built and able to be sailed or rowed.

Magnetic compass Instrument using the earth's magnetic field to indicate north and south.

Mainmast Tallest and strongest mast, in the middle of a ship.

Mizzenmast The rearmost mast of a sailing ship.

Orlop The lowest deck of a sailing ship, where the ship's cables were coiled and where, in battle, wounded men were carried for treatment.

Periscope Long retractable tube containing reflecting lenses and prisms, giving vision above the surface from inside a submerged submarine.

Port 1. Left-hand side of a ship, facing forward; 2. Square or round hole cut in a ship's side for daylight, access, or the firing of guns.

Roundship General name for a cargo-carrying ship (distinct from a "long ship," or fighting galley) from Greek times to the 15th century.

Rudder Hinged timber or plate on a ship's stern, for changing the ship's direction.

Trireme Greek oared galley with three banks of oars.

Yacht Originally a state vessel for carrying kings, princes, and ambassadors; today, any sail or powered vessel used for pleasure and not plying for hire.

INDEX